Maps

CULTURES
IN
COLLISION

CULTURES IN COLLISION

The Boxer Rebellion

———•———

WILLIAM J. DUIKER

PRESIDIO PRESS
SAN RAFAEL, CALIFORNIA
LONDON, ENGLAND

Copyright© 1978 by Presidio Press

Published by Presidio Press of San Rafael, California,
and London, England, with editorial offices at
1114 Irwin Street, San Rafael, California

Library of Congress Cataloging in Publication Data

Duiker, William J   1932 –
  Cultures in collision.

  Bigliography: p.
  Includes index.
  1. Boxers.   2. Nationalism — China.   3. China —
  History — 1900.   I. Title.
DS771.D84   951'.03   77-73550
ISBN 0-89141-028-7

Cover illustration by Karl O. Lichtenstein

Printed in the United States of America

To my favorite daughters,
Laura and Claire

Contents

Illustrations

Acknowledgements

In the course of writing this book I received assistance and encouragement from a number of sources. To Joyce Eakin and Richard Sommers of the Military History Archives at the Army War College, I would like to express my appreciation for introducing me to the files on the Boxer Rebellion contained in the Spanish-American Survey. I am also indebted to the staffs of the Orientalia Division at the Library of Congress and at the Archives in the Ministry of Foreign Affairs in Paris, and to Mr. Li Nien-hsüan at the Academia Sinica at Nankang, Taiwan, for helping me to locate useful archival sources.

Thanks are also due to Leon Stout of the Penn State Room in Pattee Library at The Pennsylvania State University for assisting me in selecting the photographs used in this book, and to Mrs. Karen Zwigart for her typing and editorial assistance.

Finally, I would like to thank the Institute for the Arts and Humanistic Studies, and the College Fund for Research of the College of Liberal Arts at The Pennsylvania State University for providing financial assistance in bringing this project to fruition.

As always, my deepest gratitude goes to my wife, Yvonne, for making our home such a pleasant place in which to live and work.

Introduction

For three-quarters of a century the Boxer Rebellion has captured the imaginations of readers throughout the world. To a certain extent this fascination simply reflects an enduring interest in the behavior of human beings under stress: the Boxer uprising led to one of the most horrifying news stories of modern times — the murder of dozens of Christian missionaries and the siege of the foreign diplomatic community in Peking. In the years immediately following the revolt, literally dozens of books and stories — diaries and memoirs of participants and popular accounts by journalists — appeared in Western languages, making the siege and its consequences one of the most thoroughly reported events of its day.

In recent years the impact of the Boxer Rebellion and the siege at Peking has faded as modern man finds new ways to test the endurance of his fellow creatures. A number of scholarly accounts on the origins of the crisis have appeared, and popular histories of the siege itself have been published at irregular intervals. Curiously, however, few attempts have been made in recent years to write a balanced account of the war for the general reader searching for its causes and its consequences for China and its relations with the West. This is unfortunate, because there is much more to the Boxer Rebellion than the siege at Peking and its effects on the lives of the individuals involved. The conflict represents a period of history that has an importance all its own. It is the story of two cultures on a collision course: an expanding West, vigorous, vital, and self-confident, clashing with an introverted China, tradition-bound, arrogant in its self-sufficiency, and anxious above all to be left alone. The Boxer Rebellion was not simply a struggle of arms and of governments but of contending civilizations, of two contradictory views of the world and the nature of man. The consequences were tragic. Misunderstanding escalated into hatred and bloodshed, resulting in a confrontation between China and virtually the whole Western world.

For Americans, the Boxer Rebellion is particularly noteworthy, for it marks a significant stage in the rise to prominence of the United States in Asia. The uprising led to America's first land war in Asia and its first military action taken in conjunction with other Western powers. As such, the conflict was a brief forecast of things to come. Like the period after World War II when the United States attempted to play a decisive role in the affairs of China, it demonstrated some of the inherent contradictions in America's foreign policy in Asia—contradictions which still exist in our own day. In a very real sense, then, the Boxer Rebellion marks the beginning of the present revolutionary century in Asia.

Yet the modern reader, learning today about the causes of the Boxer Rebellion, is likely to conclude that the world has come a long way since 1900. China is now master of its own fate and a central political and military force in East Asia. Foreign nations no longer possess massive territorial concessions on the China mainland, Christian missionaries no longer dream of converting millions of Chinese, and the myth of the China market is no longer an active enticement to the Western businessman. In short, today the behavior of the Western powers during the crisis seems petty and almost incomprehensible.

Before we become too arrogant in our condescending view of our ancestors, it is worth reflecting on our own experience. The cultural misunderstanding which led to the Boxer Rebellion has not dissipated in our own time and is a major factor in creating the gap that still exists between the West and China. The Boxer uprising was the first truly spontaneous reaction of the Chinese people to the growing Western presence in China, and the intense hostility of the rebels stunned Western observers there, most of whom were almost totally unaware of the resentment their activities had aroused. Now, over half a century later, China has again rejected the West, and again we have not yet fully understood why.

The repetition of the pattern carries a sobering message with dangerous implications for the future. Today, as in 1900, we are paying a price for our failure to understand the Chinese people and the causes of the deep resentments they have held against the West. Hopefully, reexamining the Boxer Rebellion — seemingly so distant now in time — will help to shed light on the relationship between these two great cultures.

Chapter One

Worlds in Collision

For nearly two thousand years the dominant position of China in East Asia was unquestioned. Centrally located on the highly populated eastern rim of the Eurasian land mass, the Chinese empire emerged in history in the final centuries of the pre-Christian era and gradually assumed a major role in the international affairs of the Western Pacific. Two of China's great dynasties, the Han and the T'ang, concentrated on land expansion and spread southward into Southeast Asia, westward into Central Asia (with expeditions going as far as the Caspian Sea), and northward to the southern edge of the vast Gobi Desert in Outer Mongolia.

Over the centuries the force of Chinese expansion was irresistible, and by the rise of the Ming dynasty in the fourteenth century the Chinese empire extended from the Red River delta in the south to Manchuria in the north, and from the borders of Tibet and Turkestan in the west to the China Sea in the east. Under the Ming (1369-1644), China for a time even entertained thoughts of becoming a sea power. In the early fifteenth century the imperial court dispatched naval expeditions to the Indianized states of Southeast

1

Asia, the Indian subcontinent, and as far as the Red Sea and the eastern coast of Africa. The primary motive for the voyages was apparently trade, rather than political domination, but they marked the growing influence of the Chinese empire in the southern seas as well as along its western and northern frontiers. Generally, China's interest in neighboring countries lay in political influence and border security, rather than outright military conquest or extension of territory. For this reason, China was normally satisfied to establish a tributary relationship with its smaller neighbors, guaranteeing peace and security in a mutually amicable relationship. Except for Vietnam, which for a thousand years was treated as a military province of China, the imperial court rarely ventured militarily beyond the southern border with Southeast Asia, except to avenge an insult or to protect the patrimony of a friendly ruler.

Chinese power was not always invincible. Occasionally the empire was attacked and even conquered — by the Mongols in the thirteenth century and by the Manchus four hundred years later. Foreign conquest did not necessarily disrupt the traditional pattern, for the new rulers normally adopted existing institutions and customs and were gradually absorbed into Chinese society. In any event, the primacy of China in Asia was not questioned — certainly not by the Chinese themselves, whose very name for China (Chung Kuo, or the Central Kingdom) strongly implied a central position in human affairs. For the most part, China's neighbors acknowledged its suzerainty in return for trading privileges, the Chinese emperor's recognition of the legitimacy of a fellow ruler, and occasionally Chinese protection against internal or external enemies. If the tribute system, by which all of its neighbors were linked to China through ties of fealty and allegiance, was an advantage to China, it provided benefits for neighboring countries as well.[1]

In the sixteenth century this Sinocentric cultural universe was shaken by arrivals from the West. Early Western visitors to China — for the most part traders or missionaries —

wanted to establish trading relations with the Chinese empire or preach the Christian religion to the "heathen Chinee." Limited by their numbers and by the vastness of the empire, they had a realistic idea of the obstacles involved and apparently did not aspire to carry out their operations on a large scale. The missionaries, usually Jesuits, Franciscans, or Dominicans, undoubtedly hoped to change Chinese religious practices and those social habits which were considered incompatible with Christianity, but they had no desire to overthrow the empire or to change Chinese political and social institutions as a whole. Early Western visitors either were indifferent to the culture or actually admired Chinese ways—the courtesy and intelligence of the leaders, and the industry and peacefulness of the people.

Western involvement in China was thus limited, and the feeling was mutual. China itself had no particular interest in things Western. Aside from a passing fascination with the scientific gadgetry proudly displayed by early Jesuit missionaries, the Chinese saw few benefits from connections with the West. Eventually they began to view Western ideas as a threat to their culture: Western commerce eroded Chinese self-sufficiency and depleted local currency; Western religion, avowing that there was only one God and that his viceroy was in Rome, diminished the status of the Confucian ruler. When Catholic missionaries began to criticize the Chinese practice of ancestor worship as idolatrous, Chinese officials feared Christianity would weaken their people's morals. It is difficult for a Westerner today—and perhaps was virtually impossible for the Westerner of the seventeenth century — to understand that many Chinese saw Christianity as a serious threat to their way of life much as a modern American might view communism. In general, the Jesuits attempted to minimize the disturbance of established ritual. However, such attempts were undermined by rival Catholic orders and were eventually denounced by the Vatican. By then the Chinese court had already taken steps to limit its relations with the West. Catholic missionaries were compelled to leave China, and

Western traders were restricted to one port, Canton, far from the major population centers.

Until early in the nineteenth century, then, contact between China and the West was curtailed by distance and by Chinese indifference to the outside world. For a long time, preoccupied by problems and interests elsewhere, Europe acquiesced and allowed its relations with China to stagnate. By the early years of the nineteenth century, however, new circumstances altered Europe's perception of its interests in Asia. The Industrial Revolution simultaneously created new needs and new opportunities—a rising demand for raw materials which European nations could not themselves supply, and competition for consumer markets which could absorb the increasing output of European factories. To meet the challenge of a growing commercial economy, Western merchants began once again to look to Asia and its wealth of oil, tin, rubber and other natural resources, and particularly to China with its 400 million potential customers.

Great Britain was the leader in the struggle to open China to Western trade. For a century the British had suffered a trade imbalance with China as the Chinese had refused to buy English goods in return for the export of Chinese tea to England. By the end of the eighteenth century the British had found a commodity to recoup currency losses to China: opium. Grown in northern India and shipped to south China by the East India Company, opium became so popular in China that by the first quarter of the new century the currency flow had reversed. The Chinese government attempted to stop the importation of opium, claiming, with some justification, that it had a deleterious effect on the health and morale of the Chinese peasant. In a famous letter to the young Queen Victoria, a Chinese official, Lin Tse-hsü, wrote:

Let us ask, where is your conscience? I have heard that the smoking of opium is very strictly forbidden by your country; that is because the harm caused by opium is clearly understood. Since it is not permitted to do harm to your own country, then even less should you let it be passed on to the harm of other countries—how much less to China! Of all that China exports to foreign countries, there is not a single thing which is not beneficial to people; they are of benefit when eaten, or of benefit when used, or of benefit when resold; all are beneficial. Is there a single article from China which has done any harm to foreign countries?[2]

England, however, was not persuaded. In the view of British officials in London and of merchants in Birmingham, Glasgow, and Manchester, the issue was not opium but freedom of trade. If the Chinese would open their doors to Western commerce and permit Western firms to sell their wares without hindrance throughout the empire, there would be no need for shippers to sell opium in China, and the problem would resolve itself.

The imperial court, however, was determined to suppress the opium trade. This position led in 1839 to war with Britain, a humiliating military setback, and the resulting peace treaty of 1842 compelled the Chinese to open selected coastal ports to Western trade. The Opium War decisively changed the course of Asian history. In succeeding decades the Western presence increased as China was gradually forced to open its villages and towns to foreign commercial activities, not only in so-called treaty ports, but in the interior as well.

Where Western merchants trod, missionaries were not far behind. The great missionary explosion of the sixteenth and seventeenth centuries had come primarily from the Catholic countries—France, Italy, and Spain. During the nineteenth century, when a revival of religious fervor swept Great Britain and the United States, the Protestant nations began to take the lead. Missionary groups throughout the Western world focused their attention on the benighted Chinese peasant, and, as the merchant called for oil to light the lamps of China, the missionary called for spiritual sustenance for Chinese souls.

In the Western mind, missionary activity provided an ethical counterpoint to commercial activities in China.

If Western commerce raised the material level of Chinese civilization, then Christianity would provide spiritual uplift and justify the white man's presence in Asia. It is easy to see the Westerner as hypocritically rationalizing commercial greed with a superficial morality. Yet in the nineteenth century, interference in underdeveloped societies in Asia and Africa was considered not only inevitable but ultimately beneficial. By the last quarter of the century, Charles Darwin's theory of natural selection, of "survival of the fittest," was being applied to human societies. Thus, in the evolution of mankind, those civilizations which failed to respond to the challenges of external forces would lose the struggle for survival and would be driven off the crowded ladder of civilization. The process was relentless, and through it the species evolved.

The theory of evolution gave support to Western colonization, making it a matter of enlightened self-interest as well as cultural beneficence. Western imperialist nations felt they needed colonies in order to maintain their status as great powers. At the same time they could justify their colonial activities by considering them altruistic attempts to provide the natives with the secrets necessary to succeed in the brutal struggle for survival.

Western expansion in China, then, was motivated by a variety of factors: a commercial interest in natural resources and consumer markets; an evangelical urge to spread the gospel and the wonders of Western civilization; and a general belief that national greatness required colonies in far-flung corners of the globe. With the defeat of the Chinese by Great Britain in 1842, the waves of imperialism began to lap at the outer bulwarks of the Chinese empire. From the north and the northwest, tsarist Russia used the pretext of trade to expand into Outer Mongolia and Chinese Turkestan. In the southwest, the British gradually advanced northward from Burma and India to Tibet, where they collided with an outpost of St. Petersburg. The French, ever concerned that they might fall behind the British in the race for colonies, reacted to the British move into Burma

A typical scene inside the Tartar city, Peking (*Leslie's Weekly*, July 14, 1900, cover)

by seizing Vietnam, Laos, and Cambodia and creating a
French "balcony on the Pacific." Even China's Asian neighbor
Japan was anxious to share the spoils. In the mid-1870s
Japan staked a claim to the Ryukyu Islands, traditionally
a Chinese tributary area. A decade later Tokyo began
making gestures aimed at detaching Korea from the Chinese
empire.

In themselves, these advances did not directly threaten
the independence of China. The areas occupied or coveted
by the imperialist nations were not integral parts of the
Chinese empire, nor were their populations Chinese in race
or culture, although Korea and Vietnam had modeled their
own civilizations after the Chinese. These areas, in fact,
were the outer defenses of the Chinese state and had been
viewed as such by the Chinese for hundreds of years. Still,
stripped of the protective covering which the tributary system
had historically afforded, China would feel increasingly
vulnerable to foreign conquest.

Western advances into China during the last third of
the nineteenth century were in some respects misleading
indications of the degree of Western success in opening
Chinese society to outside influence. The volume of trade
generated with China was undoubtedly disappointing to
enthusiastic believers in the China dream. The myth of the
China market never materialized — nor has it developed to
this day. However, Western commercial interests in China
continued in other promising areas: mining, banking, and
railroad construction. By the 1880s a new type of imperialist
device had evolved, known now as the sphere of influence.
When political and social problems at midcentury
started to weaken the centralized authority of the court,
provincial governments began exerting an increasing degree
of independence. Western companies that had penetrated
into the interior of China began (sometimes with the aid of
their governments) to make special arrangements with provincial
authorities whereby they would gain monopolies
over construction and mineral rights. By the middle of the
1890s such spheres of influence, each dominated by a single

foreign power, had become commonplace in China: the British in the Yangtse Valley; the French in Yunnan and Kwangsi in the south; the Russians in Manchuria; and the Japanese in coastal Fukien. While Western governments had not yet overtly attempted to usurp administrative powers in such areas, foreign interference in Chinese affairs was on the rise and the court in Peking was increasingly powerless to stop it.

THE CHINESE RESPONSE

China was slow to respond to the growing challenge from the West. Long convinced of the innate superiority of its own institutions, China did not find it easy to accept the new vulnerability. A few intellectuals, concerned at China's defeat in the Opium War, recommended changes in the administration in Peking, but the court, now entering a long period of decline which would last beyond the end of the century, failed to see the necessity for urgent action. Even after a second defeat by Western powers in the late 1850s, the dynasty resisted change. By the 1870s progressive elements had finally and reluctantly come to the conclusion that reform was necessary. A gradual period of modernization in the military, commerce, industry, transport, and communications was initiated. A few young Chinese were sent abroad to study.

These hesitant efforts to modernize, however, could not halt the paralysis that was gradually affecting the empire. Beyond the cities, village China was virtually untouched by reform. Even the most progressive Chinese hoped that Western technology could be grafted onto the Chinese system without irreparably damaging sacred institutions and that industry and commerce could be developed without altering the country's traditional agrarian character. The attempt at restricting cultural reform primarily to economic spheres was often advantageous to the individual businessman. Ambitious Chinese made their fortunes in trade and then used their new wealth to buy land or to obtain a position in the bureaucracy. For many, Western ways were simply a tool to achieve status in the traditional sectors of society. For a generation after 1875, China hesitated between old and new, reluctant to advance but afraid to retreat.

China's failure to halt the gradual intrusion of Western culture inevitably caused a growing split over how to handle the problem. Some Chinese, exposed to Western civilization through travel abroad, contacts with missionaries and merchants, or translations of Western books, began to conclude that only major reforms, including a willingness to borrow ideas from the West, could save China from political and cultural annihilation. Such attitudes were common in the big coastal cities, but the people of the great Chinese heartland by and large resisted the idea that China must Westernize or perish. To them, China's way of life and venerated institutions must be preserved, even at the cost of continued military defeat — a Chinese equivalent of the "better dead than red" argument in Cold War America. These contrasting views were reflected at the court in Peking, where moderate reformist Chinese ministers argued for change against the stubborn resistance of conservative Manchu nobles.

This bitter controversy raging in the capital and the treaty ports along the coast had no counterpart in the towns and villages where the great mass of the Chinese population lived. Congenitally indifferent to the outside world, for a long time village China was only dimly aware of the growing cultural confrontation between China and the West. For the average Chinese, the West was represented by an occasional traveller or by those few merchants or missionaries who lived in the vicinity. Often the villager, peaceable and tolerant by nature, simply ignored the foreigner or considered him a mild curiosity. Sometimes, however, it was difficult to maintain such an attitude of easy tolerance. As the century wore on and the Western presence in China gradually increased, the effects on the daily lives of Chinese became more marked. Increased imports of Western goods, facilitated by a Western-imposed standard tariff of only five percent *ad valorem* on all imports, cut into Chinese manufactures, especially cloth goods. A large proportion of the traditional clothing of China had been provided by home handicraft producers. While cheap and sturdy, such local products had difficulty competing with the machine-made products of the West.

Another area affected by the Western presence was transport. Western consortia built railroads from Peking to Tientsin, along the Yangtse Valley, and from north China to the Yangtse River cities of Shanghai and Hankow, gradually curtailing the river junk trade which had long functioned as the major means of transporting goods. Thus, slowly but inexorably, Western commerce was beginning to disrupt the social and economic structures of Chinese civilization. As it did so, the Chinese came to see the West not as a curiosity but as a menace.

It was the missionaries, however, whose presence was most resented in China. In the last half of the nineteenth century there was a sharp rise in missionary activity in China. Until midcentury China had been almost entirely a Catholic preserve. Catholic proselytizing had begun with the arrival of Franciscans and Jesuits in the sixteenth century, while the first Protestant missionary did not arrive until almost three hundred years later. As a result of treaty agreements in 1858, however, Western Christian missionaries were allowed to travel freely and preach throughout China, and Protestant groups began to carry the gospel to the Chinese. In 1858 there were eighty-one Protestant missionaries in China, all in the southern and coastal areas. By 1889 there were over thirteen hundred scattered throughout virtually every province in China. Over fifty percent of these missionaries were from Great Britain; the bulk of the remainder came from the United States and Germany. Their activities had been rewarded with some success — an estimated fifty-five thousand Protestant converts in China.

The Catholics were still strong contenders in the competition for Chinese souls, however. By the mid-1890s there were about 750 Catholic priests in China, mostly French, with a few Italians. Because the Catholics had been active longer than the Protestants, they had achieved greater success — approximately half a million converts throughout China. The competition climaxed in the final decade of the century. By 1900 there were over 2,800 missionaries in China. They worked in every Chinese province except for the traditionally xenophobic Hunan and claimed nearly a million converts. The Catholics still predominated with 720,000 followers; the various Protestant denominations totaled over 130,000.

In retrospect, it seems obvious that such a mass of foreigners, with their alien customs and doctrines, would invite the hostility of simple farmer and suspicious scholar-gentry alike. Few of the newly arrived missionaries spoke Chinese, unlike the first Catholic arrivals, who had attempted not only to master the language but also to understand the inner nature of Chinese culture. With no knowledge of the language and little interest in Chinese civilization, the late-nineteenth-century missionaries operated under their old prejudices. Many, if not most, were contemptuous of Asian civilization and communicated their arrogance and condescension in their dealings with the Chinese. Often the missionaries themselves came from small towns and had little cosmopolitan interest in other civilizations. On arrival in China, they would install themselves in a mission compound, preserving their own way of life and isolating themselves from the native population. Often the missionaries were women, and their activities particularly excited suspicion and contempt, for the place of women in China was exclusively in the home.

The new arrivals often exacerbated the situation by their open interference in the traditional way of life. Contemptuous of local mores and justice, many went out of their way to protect their converts from legal charges levied by village authorities. To the missionary, it appeared that the non-Christian authorities deliberately harassed those who had accepted Jesus. To the local authorities and the non-

to blame for the incidents. They were convinced that many British missionaries had been overly aggressive in demanding resident rights and in protecting the interests of their converts. To avoid becoming excessively identified with the missionary elements, London instructed its diplomatic representatives to discourage British missionaries from living in the interior and to reject pleas for protection from missionary groups in such areas. Still, the British government did feel duty-bound to protect missionaries' rights once they had been established in practice. It was thus caught between the duty to protect its citizens and a reluctance to become entangled in the internal affairs of the Chinese empire.[3] Other nations, such as France and Germany, were less cautious about supporting the rights and activities of their subjects in China. When the Chinese government, itself concerned about the rise of antiforeign sentiment, asked the Western governments to place missionary activities under stricter Chinese control, foreign officials were reluctant to agree. Near the end of the century, as the tension mounted, a major confrontation seemed only a matter of time.

Chapter Two

The Climax of
Imperialism in China

I t is one of the ironies of history that throughout the last hundred years many international crises have arisen in areas of relatively limited political or economic importance to the parties involved. At the end of the nineteenth century the European powers several times came close to war over a few hundred square miles of African wasteland or over areas in Asia thousands of miles from their own borders. World War I itself was precipitated by rivalries in the Balkans, a region of minor international importance. More recently, the United States squandered its resources and its reputation in a prolonged war in a southeast Asian country few Americans had even heard of before the Geneva Conference of 1954.

The explanation, of course, lies in the international system which in recent decades has governed relations between the great powers. Since the nineteenth century the world system has been based on a balance of power between competing states. With several great powers jealously guarding their own interests, even a slight shift in the balance of power can lead to an international crisis, and sometimes to war. Given the intricate alliance relationships among the various powers, such a crisis could quickly develop into a war with global dimensions.

Over the decades the weak links in the balance-of-power mechanism have proved to be areas outside of Western civilization where the interests and ambitions of great powers collide and where no one power has yet established its influence and control. In many parts of the world — the Balkans, Africa, East and Southeast Asia—the disintegration of native authority and political and social instability created opportunities for nations seeking to increase their international interests and responsibilities. In such areas, competition among nations to establish spheres of influence was fierce, although in retrospect it is clear that the importance of such areas to the great powers was highly exaggerated.

By the last decade of the nineteenth century China had become an area where the great powers were confronting each other. Dreams of the China market had excited feverish interest in Bordeaux and Lyons, Birmingham and Manchester, Boston and Philadelphia. Visions of a warm-water port in Manchuria or north China kept Russian strategists awake in St. Petersburg. Fears of Russian expansion in northeast Asia troubled the fitful sleep of Japanese policymakers in Tokyo. Some officials resisted the "China fever," however. The British Foreign Office and the U.S. Department of State half-heartedly attempted to curtail involvement in the China question. Germany's Bismarck, until his dismissal from office in 1891, considered all Asia unworthy of the concern of a Prussian minister of state. But, although commercial dreams were slow to become realities, China's gradual political and social disintegration seemed to invite foreign intervention, and the race for spheres of influence in China climaxed as the century drew to a close. Each country reserved certain provinces or blocks of provinces for exploitation, and provincial leaders, freed from central control by the decline of power in Peking, found it increasingly convenient to deal with foreign interests — governmental or private — on their own initiative.

European commercial and political involvement in China thus developed a momentum of its own, despite the very limited real interest of the great powers in East Asia. As foreign pressure further weakened Peking, the conviction grew that the Chinese empire was on the verge of collapsing into fragmented areas directly controlled by outside powers. Frantic at the thought that they might be left behind in the rush for spoils, outside powers (even some, like Italy, heretofore indifferent to the siren call of the China market) rushed to stake a claim to Chinese territory and gazed enviously at the successes of their rivals.

In the south, British and French interests collided. Great Britain, since the Opium War, had more citizens in China than all the other European powers combined, and had staked out a zone of commercial domination in the lower Yangtse Valley. If not formally a sphere of influence, it functioned as one for all intents and purposes. In response, the French began extending their own control from their new protectorate of Vietnam into the southernmost Chinese provinces of Kwangsi, Kwangtung, and Yunnan.

In the north competition was perhaps even more intense. For decades the Russians had been the most active outside power in north China. Having gradually expanded across the Siberian steppes during the past two centuries, tsarist Russia had begun to make significant political and economic inroads in China in the mid-nineteenth century. In 1860 St. Petersburg obtained title to thousands of acres of land beyond the Amur River, hitherto regarded by China as its own. Within a generation Russian interests had penetrated Manchuria, and in 1896 Russia received the right to build a railway across the heart of the Manchurian plain to its Pacific outpost at Vladivostok. Economic and political interests naturally followed the railroad, and Russian influence began to spill over into the Korean peninsula, which was coveted by Japan. As Russian power spread across north China toward the Sea of Japan, Tokyo grew watchful and bided its time.

CLIMAX IN SHANTUNG

In 1897 events took place which were to bring the imperialist wave to a crest. Germany, a latecomer to the China land-grab, coveted a position in the Pacific. Since Bismarck's successors did not share his distaste for Asian adventures, by 1895 Germany's commercial interests in China had become second only to those of Great Britain. German military strategists had kept a sharp lookout for prospective locations for a sphere of influence or a naval coaling station. They finally settled on two possibilities: Chusan Island, off the China coast near the mouth of the Yangtse River, and the island of Formosa, long attractive to several European powers. Formosa lost its appeal when it was seized by Japan after that country defeated China in the war of 1894-1895. Since Chusan Island was technically in the general area of Britain's sphere of interest in the Yangtse Valley, China rebuffed Germany's advances, claiming that it had promised the British not to allot the strategic island to another foreign power. Germany would have to look elsewhere for its outpost in the Pacific.

By the late 1890s German attention began to focus on the Shantung Peninsula, which jutted into the North China Sea. Rocky and inhospitable, Shantung had relatively little to recommend it from a commercial point of view, but it was strategically located and its Chiao Chow Bay was an excellent location for a naval base. A further inducement was the fact that for nearly twenty years German missionaries had been operating in the interior of Shantung Province and entreating Berlin to protect their interests.

The Germans feared that the dismemberment of China could leave them without a share. Consequently, in 1895, immediately following the defeat of China by Japan, they opened talks with Peking on the possible cession of land in Shantung Province for a German naval base. Unfor-

tunately for the Germans, the Chinese government was itself becoming interested in building a naval base in Chiao
Chow Bay. Encouraged perhaps by the Russians who were
also mildly interested in the area, the Chinese refused the
German request.

The negotiations, however, had whetted the Germans'
appetite, and they were determined to find a pretext to
seize what they could not obtain by diplomatic means.
In November of 1897 the pretext presented itself when
rioting Chinese peasants murdered two German missionaries
in the interior of Shantung Province. Kaiser Wilhelm checked
briefly with Tsar Nicholas to make sure that Russia would
take no counteraction (Nicholas simply noted in the margin
of the message from the German monarch that he could
not "approve or disapprove"). The kaiser then gave his
enthusiastic assent and the Germans moved in. They occupied the area around Chiao Chow Bay and demanded
leasing rights to construct railways and mines elsewhere
in the province. With German efficiency, they soon began
to build up the area, planting trees and constructing roads,
a bathing beach, a new hotel, and even an underground
sewer system. Local Chinese suspected that the latter was
intended as an escape route for when the Chinese drove
the Germans into the sea.

In Peking several court officials who had witnessed
with growing anger the rapacity of the great powers were
inclined to strike back, regardless of the costs. Others,
however, feared that, unless China could obtain help from
other world powers — notably Russia, who had somewhat
hypocritically posed as China's friend against the other
European powers — Chinese resistance would simply spark
a land-grab that would complete the dismemberment of the
empire. The proponents of appeasement were temporarily
victorious, and agreement was reached with Germany,
primarily on the latter's terms, by January 1898.

In world capitals reaction to the German advance
into Shantung was mixed. The Russians, who had seriously
contemplated seizing Chiao Chow Bay for themselves, were

miffed that the Germans had managed a successful coup. St. Petersburg was anxious to stay on good terms with Berlin, however, and soon decided to obtain compensation elsewhere. Early in 1898 the Russians demanded and received a leasehold on Port Arthur at the tip of the Liaotung Peninsula. This request for Port Arthur was ironic in that Russia had blocked Japan's attempt to seize the same area at the end of the Sino-Japanese War. As a year-round warm-water port and a gateway to the vast mineral riches of Manchuria, Port Arthur had the potential to become the keystone of a new Russian empire in north China.

London was concerned at Germany's move as well as Russia's response. Although British commercial interests agitated for immediate action, the government was reluctant to take a firm position. It feared that a strong response might precipitate the final collapse of the Chinese empire, a development which would not benefit Great Britain. Deciding that the situation in north China did not warrant military action, the British limited themselves to requesting a lease for a coaling station at Weihaiwei on the tip of the Shantung peninsula. That the request was directed primarily against the Russians was indicated by the terms of the agreement—the British leasehold was to last as long as that of the Russians in Port Arthur, twenty-five years.

There were reactions, too, from other powers. The French demanded and received the bay of Kwang Chow Wan in south Kwangtung Province. The Italians put in a bid for San Men Bay. One Peking official commented scornfully, "They don't even wait until they have a pretext before they make their demands!" To many, within China and without, it seemed as if the final death anguish of the Manchu dynasty was at hand.

Perhaps the most significant reaction to the German seizure of Chiao Chow Bay and the land-grab that followed came from the United States. From the beginning the American attitude toward Western behavior in China had been ambivalent. On the one hand traditional American

Cartoon entitled "The Dragon's Choice" (*Harper's Weekly*, August 18, 1900, cover)

anticolonialism and suspicion of the motives of the Old World led many to criticize European imperialism and sympathize with its victims. On the other hand the United States for many years had maintained commercial interests in China and had been perfectly happy to accept the trading advantages which accrued from the increasing Western pressure on China. Moreover, American missionaries in China formed one of the more vocal groups lobbying for an activist foreign policy in Asia. The number of American missionaries in China had nearly doubled during the 1890s, to more than a thousand by the end of the century.

The tension in America due to its China policy was evident in its behavior as the situation rose to a crisis. The McKinley administration, as well as the man in the street, was repelled by the rapacious seizure of Chinese territory by the imperialist powers. In 1898 the American minister to China, Charles Denby, recommended to Washington that the United States officially protest the dismemberment of the Chinese empire. Yet there were signs of support for American imperialism. Spokesmen for commercial interests advocated a foreign policy that would actively protect Yankee business concerns in China. Missionary groups clamored for official protection by American diplomatic representatives. And the strains of *realpolitik* had begun to be heard in the United States. With American commercial interests on the rise, the United States gradually became involved in the balance-of-power game, and those with a financial stake in the policy came to accept its rules. American participation in the exploitation of China was extolled as natural and inevitable. Some justified an activist policy by claiming that the United States was simply bearing the "white man's burden." Others considered imperialism to be its own justification. Illustrative is an article entitled "Expansion Unavoidable" in *Harper's Weekly*:

If history teaches anything, it is that conservatism when it prevails habitually indicates national decay. As stagnant water breeds the microbe of death, so nature itself preaches action, and in national life action is synonymous with progress. The people of the United States, known for their restless energy, which possesses the boy not yet out of his teens equally with the man who has reached or passed the allotted threescore years and ten, are expanding constantly. It is by this innate spirit of expansion that the marvellous wealth of our time was created.

Since, then, our trade with China has even now assumed such gigantic proportions as to call for a written guarantee of non-interference, the United States must be prepared to defend its vested rights on the other side of the Pacific. In order to be able to do so, territorial acquisition, or territorial expansion, is a necessity. There is no other alternative; it is either, Renounce expansion of commerce, or Be prepared to defend it. Only a naturally weak nation or one strong but unprepared is likely to be attacked. Physical strength always imposes respect, with individuals as well as with nations. The old adage, In time of peace prepare for war, is as true now as it ever was. [1]

Concrete evidence of the growing imperialist trend in American foreign policy appeared in 1898. Taking advantage of the war with Spain, American forces seized the Philippines and, despite the fact that rebellious Filipino forces had already declared the islands a republic, transformed them into an American colony. His decision, President William McKinley explained, had been motivated by moral concern. More realistically, perhaps, the Philippines were attractive for their economic value. To the new American minister-designate to China, Edwin Conger, the Philippines were a stepping-stone to the China market. Ironically, two years later there were those who advocated an activist American foreign policy in China as a means of protecting our investment in the Philippines.

THE OPEN DOOR NOTES

American foreign policy at the turn of the century thus reflected the conflicting attitudes of two centuries: traditional anticolonialism versus economic imperialism, a natural sympathy for the underdog versus a belief in the white man's burden. This mixture of sentiments was reflected in the attitude of U.S. Secretary of State John Hay. Like many of his countrymen, Hay was unhappy at the land seizures which had been launched in late 1897. On the other hand, he was pressured by commercial and missionary interests to undertake an active role in the China crisis. When American naval interests voiced their desire to obtain a coaling station on the coast of Fukien Province, Secretary Hay was mildly favorable to the request, protesting only its timing. Nor did he dispute the contention that commerce was America's main interest in China.

Though some elements in American society called for greater involvement in China, the nature of American interests there diverged in important respects from those of such powers as France, Russia, and Germany. Whereas the needs of the latter seemed to lie in the establishment of commercial and economic monopolies in a given area, thus limiting their interest to clearly defined spheres of influence, American commercial groups seemed more anxious to open all of China to free trade conditions. For this reason, and because of America's moral sympathy for China, Secretary Hay issued the now famous Open Door Notes of September 1899. Although advised by some to accept the spheres of influence as an "established fact," Hay was finally persuaded to state the general principles of American foreign policy in China and ask the great powers for their adherence. The first note called for a gentleman's agreement among the powers to preserve the territorial integrity of China. It did not require the imperialist powers to abandon their spheres of influence but asked them to make a distinction between freedom of trade, under which all nations would have equal rights throughout China, regardless of individual spheres of influence, and special interests for mining and investment. The spheres of influence were thus acknowledged, but their scope was to be carefully circumscribed.

Responses from the powers showed a variety of attitudes. The British feared the consequences of a divided China, and their interests, like those of the United States, lay in maximizing trading opportunities; they were delighted. The French and Germans responded carefully, stating in effect that they would concur if others did also. The Russians, against whose activities in Manchuria the notes seemed primarily directed, sent the most ambiguous reply, declaring that their previous actions had adequately demonstrated their adherence to a policy of "open door." (To many observers, this was a dubious statement.) More significantly, the Russian reply totally ignored a major point in Hay's note: that the powers agree not to charge discriminatory rates against the goods of other foreign powers on rail lines in its sphere of influence. This point was a specific expression of the Open Door policy; by ignoring it St. Petersburg essentially rejected the note's principles.

The Russian rejection, according to a sympathetic observer, was dictated primarily by economic motives. Andrew Malozemoff, whose *Russian Far Eastern Policy, 1881-1904* is one of the standard works in the field, claims that, since Russia was the only power which had begun to construct railways in China on a large scale, the principle of nondiscriminatory rates itself amounted to a form of discrimination and could be considered hostile to Russia. In his view the Russians had sound reasons for applying discriminatory rates on their Manchurian rail system since, unlike their Western rivals, all of their commerce came by land, rather than by sea. According to Malozemoff, Russian acceptance of Hay's note "would have been disastrous to Russian financial and economic interests in Manchuria. The doctrine as applied to Russia in the Far East was much too one-sided."[2]

It was the Russian finance minister, Sergius Witte, who pointed out to Foreign Minister Nikolai Muraviev the implications of the Open Door Note, and it was presumably at his instigation that the reference to discriminatory rates was deliberately left out of the Russian reply. Malozemoff points out that, since several of the powers agreed to respect the principles in Hay's circular only if all the other powers did likewise, the note was in effect rejected by them when the Russians refused to comply. Secretary Hay, however, took the disparate responses as a general agreement and declared in a second note in March 1900 that the Open Door was now accepted as "final and definitive."

For decades the Open Door Notes were viewed as the cornerstone of American foreign policy in East Asia. To succeeding generations of Americans they appeared to be a perfect synthesis of American morality and economic

self-interest — directed at protecting the basic rights of the
Chinese people, while at the same time coaxing the empire
gently into the mainstream of the modern world. At the
time they reflected the twofold nature of American interests in China, but they did not clarify the ambiguity in
American policy as evidenced by the administration's
response to the request for a coaling station. President
McKinley approved the request, and Secretary Hay himself
appeared mildly favorable but noted, in an understatement,
that the moment was inopportune for America to start
land-grabbing. Hay's compunctions notwithstanding, the
major obstacle to the station turned out to be Japan,
which maintained that Fukien lay in Japan's sphere of
influence. The project was dropped.

THE CHINESE RESPONSE

The events touched off by the German seizure of
Chiao Chow Bay in late 1897 led to a re-examination of
foreign policy strategy at the Manchu court in Peking.
After Western pressure on China intensified during the
middle years of the century, the Chinese government had
begun to experiment with various ways of coping with the
foreigners. They had tried ignoring them, promoting internal reform along traditional lines, maintaining a policy of
compromise and conciliation, resisting forcefully, and
playing off one power against another. Generally, none of
these policies had worked very well, and this must have
been painfully evident to the Chinese policy-makers. By
the last quarter of the century, however, once the pattern
of Western pressure had been established, Peking was
stressing the conciliatory approach, while attempting to
maximize its advantages by balancing one jealous rival
against the others. Simultaneously, half-hearted efforts
were made to modernize China's military services in the
hope that at some future date it could confront an aggressive imperialist power. The conciliatory approach was used
in a variety of circumstances — land seizures, foreign re-

diverse needs of the community—food, health and sanitation, distribution of labor, fuel supply, water, and fire defense. A parent committee, the General Committee, under the American missionary Tewkesbury, was formed to advise Minister MacDonald.

The most vital problem was maintaining a defense perimeter adequate to protect the legations from outside attack. To some degree, the buildings in the quarter could be used as a bulwark. But the streets offering access into the area needed to be sealed off, and stout barricades had to be built which could withstand cannon fire from the Chinese while allowing the defenders to fire outside. With respect to these problems the foreigners were fortunate. Responsibility for fortifications was handled by a committee under another American missionary, Dr. Frank Gamewell, who had been educated as an engineer at Cornell University before entering the missionary service. According to accounts of the siege, Gamewell was superb at his job. Under his supervision the community set to work to provide for its own safety. Here, as nowhere else, the spirit of cooperation and innovation was demonstrated. In response to Gamewell's call for sandbags, sandbags, and more sandbags, the more resourceful women in the community sewed sandbag casings out of whatever fabric was available in the area—clothing, silk and brocade furnishings, and draperies. The women manufactured an average of two thousand sandbags a day, fifty thousand over the entire period of the siege.

Another serious problem was food and water. The foodstocks of the legations were inadequate to withstand a long siege. Fortunately, there were several local grain retail shops within the quarter, and their supplies of wheat and rice were requisitioned for the duration. Such luxuries as meat and vegetables were soon in short supply, and before long the community began to slaughter its horses and mules for food. As for water, there were eight wells within the legation area. While the water was not especially clean, it could be made potable by boiling.

The "International Gun," an artillery piece constructed and used with great effectiveness by the legations during the siege at Peking (*Leslie's Weekly*, December 15, 1900, cover)

quests for mining and railway rights, and issues raised by the presence of Western missionaries in the interior of China.

Occasionally, elements at court or in the provinces had advocated a more militant response to Western encroachments, even at the risk of war. Proponents of this aggressive approach sometimes supported rapid modernization as well, but more often they contended that all forms of Western influence should be rejected as harmful to traditional institutions and values. This policy of militant traditionalism was seldom put into practice for the simple reason that it was not an effective means of dealing with the well-armed foreigners. However, as the conciliatory method itself showed signs of wear and tear, the militant conservatives were heartened to try again.

The conflict between alternatives, of course, reflected the split at court between those who felt that at least some changes would be necessary if China were to survive and those who felt that traditional institutions and customs were to be defended at all costs, even in the face of military defeat. Until the events of 1897 and 1898, the advocates of gradual reform had for long had the upper hand at the court in Peking. But the humiliating concessions made in those two years demonstrated to some the bankruptcy of the policy of moderation and compromise. More insistently, voices began to call for basic changes in Chinese foreign policy. Some officials reacted to the German demands by seeking help from Germany's traditional rivals, England and Russia, but their efforts were undermined by those countries' own demands for territorial compensation. When the German military attacks occurred, the Manchu court reluctantly began to react to the growing internal criticism of foreign encroachment. Governor Yü Hsien of Shantung was instructed to prepare local military forces for possible armed action against the Germans, and Yü Lu, the governor of Chihli Province, was ordered to station troops at Tientsin for a possible defense of the capital area. The hardening attitude in Peking, though not yet trans-

lated into action, was an indication that a number of the
more militant figures in China were gaining power. These
included Jung Lu, commander of all military forces in
north China; the Manchu nobles K'ang Yi and Prince Tuan;
General Tung Fu-hsiang, commander of the Kansu army;
and Li Ping-heng, ex-governor of Shantung and a man
noted for his antiforeign attitudes (Li was governor at the
time of the murder of the two German missionaries, and
Berlin felt he had been sympathetic to the antiforeign
outburst. At the German government's demand, the court
had declared him henceforth ineligible for high office. By
1899, however, he was a popular figure at court). Generally,
Chinese officials tended to be more moderate, the Manchu
nobles more militant.

The antiforeign militants were not the only advocates
of change in Chinese policy. For several years reformists
among low-level bureaucrats and young scholar-gentry had
begun to contend that only comprehensive institutional
reform could save the country. Until the final years of the
century they had held little sway among the policy-makers
in Peking. But in the spring of 1898, using the events of
the preceding year as yet another example of the failure
of gradual reform, the reformists renewed their efforts at
persuading the court to introduce aspects of Western culture into Chinese society. Leader of this faction was
K'ang Yu-wei, a young Confucian scholar from Kwangtung
Province in south China. Convinced of the need to start
at the top, K'ang addressed several petitions to the young
emperor, Kuang Hsü, urging major reforms in order to preserve the independence of China.

For a time it appeared that K'ang Yu-wei's attempt to
enlist the emperor's support might succeed. Kuang Hsü,
who was twenty-three years old in 1898, had only recently
come to power. Progressive, well-meaning, and open to
outside ideas, Kuang Hsü had been distressed at the course
of international events. He was attracted to K'ang's proposals and invited the young reformist to visit the imperial
palace to discuss his ideas. K'ang was evidently even more

persuasive in person, for in the summer of 1898 he helped the young emperor to prepare a series of wide-ranging edicts designed to reform the vast and antiquated bureaucracy. During the course of several weeks, decrees were issued that ordered drastic fundamental changes in such areas as education, administration, and justice.

There was a major flaw in the reformers' tactics, however. The real power in Peking lay not in the emperor's hands but in those of the aging empress dowager, Tz'u Hsi. Born to the family of an impoverished Manchu noble in 1835, the young Tz'u Hsi had been selected as a concubine for the emperor Hsien Feng. Tough-minded and astute, she had quickly learned how to protect her interests at court. After Hsien Feng's death in 1872 she was named regent for her son T'ung Chih. When he died in 1875, she retained her influence under his successor and was named empress dowager for the new emperor, her three-year-old nephew Kuang Hsü. On reaching his maturity Kuang Hsü took power, but Tz'u Hsi's influence remained crucial.

When Kuang Hsü came under the influence of K'ang Yu-wei's reformism, Tz'u Hsi resented being passed over and quickly turned hostile to the new faction. Kuang Hsü gradually became aware that forces in the capital were scheming to scuttle his reform program and turned to the commander of the Peiyang Army at Tientsin, General Yüan Shih-k'ai, to remove Tz'u Hsi from power. Yüan, an effective administrator as well as the creator of China's first modernized army, was reputed to be moderately progressive in his views toward reform and toward the foreign powers. Yüan was also a realist, however, and he quickly noted the weakness of the reformers' position. While ostensibly agreeing to help Kuang Hsü, Yüan instead informed Tz'u Hsi's confidant, Jung Lu, of the emperor's plans. When word reached Tz'u Hsi, she mustered her own forces and drove the progressives from their positions of influence. Six reformers were executed, although K'ang Yu-wei himself managed to flee to Japan. The young

Prince Tuan, Manchu reactionary (*Leslie's Weekly,* July 28, 1900, p. 64)

emperor, Kuang Hsü, was imprisoned on an island in the palace grounds. With Tz'u Hsi again firmly in control, rumors circulated that Kuang Hsü was terminally ill and about to abdicate.

Thus the conservative faction had managed to restore its power at court. Jung Lu, who had briefly held the post of viceroy of Chihli, was now named grand secretary in Peking, while retaining his command of all Chinese military forces in north China. In Shantung Province the moderate governor Chang Ju-mei was replaced by the militant Manchu xenophobe, Yü Hsien, who had been a justice in the province under the previous governor, Li Ping-heng.

It did not take long for the militants to strike at the top. Kuang Hsü's apostasy in supporting the progressives and plotting against the empress dowager could not be forgiven, and the conservatives now attempted to force his abdication. They intended to replace him with young P'u Chün, the son of the reactionary Manchu Prince Tuan. The plot failed, however, due to protests from foreign diplomats and influential Chinese officials in the provinces, including Liu K'un-yi, viceroy of Nanking. As compensation, Prince Tuan was able to have his son declared heir apparent early in 1900, as Kuang Hsü's "illness" continued.

The new conservative trend immediately surfaced in the arena of foreign policy. Angered at the Italian government's request for a naval station at San Men Bay, the court decided to refuse further concessions. The Italian demand was rejected. Viceroy Liu K'un-yi was directed to repel any Italian military advances and was given a free hand to take whatever action was necessary. Faced with this surprisingly tough Chinese response, the Italians abandoned their claim.

This new toughness at court reflected a rising wave of antiforeign sentiment in the country as a whole. Throughout the spring and summer of 1898 riots against foreigners occurred in several provinces, usually beginning as attacks on railways or missionary compounds. The discontent was centered in Shantung Province, scene of the recent German takeover. For months Western missionaries in the southern districts of the province had been seeking official protection against anti-Christian agitation, sparking resentment among local officials and villagers. Other factors soon made the situation explosive. The Germans took a heavy-handed approach to obtaining land rights along the railroad right-of-way from Tsingtao, in the newly leased Chiao Chow area, to Tsinan, capital of the province. Attacks on construction sites along the railway therefore rose in number and intensity. Then, to add to the problems, bad weather resulted in crop failure for the already impoverished peasants in the province.

According to some observers, the antiforeign unrest in the countryside was not totally spontaneous but reflected the attitudes of those in power in Peking and authorities in the districts and provinces. Whether or not this was the case, antimissionary agitation was certainly on the rise as 1899 drew to a close, particularly in Shantung Province, where Governor Yü Hsien appeared increasingly reluctant to suppress anti-Christian riots. Signs of a major confrontation between China and the West were surfacing with ominous frequency.

Chapter Three

The Rise of the Boxers

As the century drew to a close, the convergence of several factors was leading inexorably to a crisis in China's relationship with the West. The rapid disintegration of power in China had not only whetted the appetites of the great powers, but also had increased their fears that their rivals would profit from a dismemberment of the empire. On a local level, Western residents in China—missionaries in the provinces, merchants in the treaty ports, diplomats in Peking—had reacted to the land-grab with increased contempt for the Chinese people and their institutions. Their demands for special privileges were a local counterpoint to the large-scale land seizures by the great powers on the national level.

The Chinese are traditionally a tolerant and peace-loving people, accustomed to hardship, oppression, and even foreign conquest. Rarely had they given vent to their feelings in physical action. Suspicion of foreigners had always been common in Chinese villages, but antiforeign incidents had been surprisingly rare, considering the ever-growing presence of missionaries in the countryside. Now, however, Western insensitivity inevitably was having its effects and a sense of desperation was beginning to grow. The latest land seizures by the Western powers not only increased the Chinese sense of humiliation, but also made the collapse of the Chinese empire and the destruction of Chinese civilization real possibilities. Rumors circulated among Chinese as well as foreigners that the partition of the country among the various powers was only a matter of time. In late 1898 China responded at the national level by creating a new leadership determined to resist any further foreign encroachments. At the local level, villagers retaliated with increasing attacks on missionaries and other symbols of the foreign presence.

Had another factor not intervened, this wave of anti-foreign sentiment might have passed without a major crisis. The great powers, as evidenced by their reaction to John Hay's Open Door Note of 1899, had no particular desire to divide China among themselves. Indeed, many statesmen in world capitals were reluctant to take actions that might trigger the final collapse of the Chinese empire. If the court at Peking had been able to restore its territorial integrity and internal sovereignty without significantly affecting foreign trade, building, and missionary activity, most of the powers would probably have acquiesced with a considerable degree of relief.

The new militancy in Peking, then, was not by itself sufficient cause for the rising crisis in relations between China and the outside world. The catalytic force that plummeted China into the throes of war came from the villages of north China, where thousands of angry peasants unleashed the fury of their frustrations in an attack on Westerners that was unprecedented in its fierceness. Never in China's three centuries of acquaintance with the West had such an incident occurred. Rising anti-Western sentiment alone did not adequately account for the ferocity of the outburst. In the last years of the century disastrous climatic conditions had created unusual hardship for farmers throughout the empire, and particularly in central and north China. Since 1898 bad weather had seriously affected the grain harvest in the lower provinces of the Yangtse Valley, and floods throughout the area had made thousands, perhaps millions, homeless. In the north, the Yellow River had burst its banks every year since 1896. Finally, in the spring of 1900 a severe drought in the flatland area stretching from the Gulf of Chihli to the provinces of Shansi and Honan threatened crop failure in the breadbasket area of north China. For millions of Chinese peasants, hunger and starvation became tragic realities.

Historically, bad weather conditions in the rural areas of China had been followed by revolts against the established order, and the year 1900 was no exception. What was unique, however, was the conjunction of economic crisis and an active campaign against the Western invader. In the minds of superstitious peasants, the two factors became inextricably linked. Foreigners, who had angered local spirits by disrupting graveyards to build railroads and churches, were blamed for the bad weather that afflicted China. As one broadside put it,

The arrival of calamities is because of the foreign devils. They have come to China to propagate their teachings, to build telegraph lines and to construct railways. They do not believe in spirits and they desecrate the gods. It is the desire of the gods to cut up the telegraph lines, to rip up the railroads, and to cut off the heads of the foreign devils.[1]

A popular rumor in north China predicted that rain would fall if the Chinese cut off the heads of the foreign devils. Thus two problems were to be solved at one swoop.

Out of a gripping economic crisis, then, arose the specter of a vast and sacred war against the foreigner, of armies of refugees roaming the countryside, searching for food and seeking scapegoats for their afflictions. The peasantry of north China threatened to become a desperate, primitive force, bent on ridding the nation of its oppressors.

The exact origins of the Boxer movement, that vast antiforeign offensive which suddenly sprang up in villages and towns throughout north China in late 1899 and 1900, have long been disputed. Some scholars argue that the Boxers — named, apparently, for the Chinese boxing ritual performed by the adherents in preparation for action — emerged from the countless secret societies which for centuries had proliferated among poor and illiterate peasants. The origins of these secret societies — the White Lotus, the Triads, the Eight Trigrams, the Elder Brother Society, the Big Knife Society — are shrouded in legend. Most were composed of local peasants who banded together for security against bandits, rapacious landlords, and corrupt officials. Sometimes the societies were tolerated by the local authorities, but not infrequently they had an antidynastic coloration and were suppressed. Several were primitive nationalistic cliques formed to drive out the foreign rulers — the Mongols in the thirteenth century, the Manchus in the modern period. Ideologically, the secret societies were usually fairly primitive. Often the members shared a belief in local spirits and practiced secret rituals and incantations, such as the ritualized boxing (similar to the contemporary *T'ai-chi-ch'uan*), to knit together the group and guarantee themselves long life or immortality.

Secret societies had existed in Shantung Province in north China for centuries and had caused considerable difficulty to the Manchu dynasty throughout much of the nineteenth century. Organizations practicing ritual boxing had been common in the area since the 1700s, but no major society going by the name of Boxers (in Chinese, *I-ho-ch'uan,* "righteous harmonious fists") had appeared in the area until 1899. At that time local peasant groups calling themselves Boxers seemed to spring up spontaneously throughout the province. A local Chinese magistrate, Lao Nai-hsüan, published a study of the movement, claiming that it originated in the antidynastic societies which had long existed throughout the area. By extension, therefore, the movement could be considered not only anti-Western, but also anti-Manchu.

Those who locate the origins of the Boxers in the

antidynastic secret societies do not believe that the court was directly responsible for the events leading to the antiforeign movement at the turn of the century. However, many foreigners living in China during the period of the Boxer revolt felt that the court, and the empress dowager herself, had actively connived to promote the Boxer agitation. In 1927 *China and the Occident,* a serious study of the Boxer revolt by George N. Steiger, carried this assumption to its logical conclusion. Steiger contended that the Boxers did not develop out of anti-Manchu secret societies, but were a volunteer militia deliberately created by the court to resist the foreigners.[2] He argued that the name "Boxers" (*I-ho-ch'uan*) was simply a popular play on the actual name *I-ho-t'uan* ("righteous harmonious militia") and referred to the adherents' use of Boxer-like rituals. These ritual drills, Steiger claimed, were actually a Chinese adaptation of Western military drills.

Recent evidence, however, clearly shows that the Boxers were not, as Steiger claimed, simply a village militia formed at the behest of the court in Peking. The government did call for the formation of local militia at about the time the Boxers were beginning to appear, but there is no indication that the two groups were related. Indeed, the aim of the militia was to suppress local disorder, not to exacerbate it.[3] While the court can be charged with using the Boxers for its own purposes at a later stage, it cannot legitimately be accused of creating the movement.

It is probable, though not definitely established, that the Boxers were, in fact, a type of secret society formed in reaction to missionary activity, imperialist expansion, and the starvation and discontent rampant in the countryside. The movement may have originally been antidynastic in tone, but, as it grew, the court began to discern its utility in focusing antiforeign sentiment. At that point the throne attempted to shape the Boxers into militia-type organizations and to assimilate them (usually without success) into the established military framework.

Whatever its specific origins, it is clear that the Boxer

movement was both a product of antiforeign or anti-Christian feeling and a response to economic conditions. The two were related since the Boxers often seemed to believe that, if the foreigners could be driven from China, conditions would improve. In the beginning the movement was probably local and spontaneous, without centralized leadership, erupting in the villages and spreading rapidly among poor peasants, merchants, unemployed soldiers, and Buddhist monks. According to some reports, most active Boxers were adolescents, but there is evidence that, particularly as conservatives came to power in Peking, some local officials and scholar-gentry began to offer their support and encouragement.

Organizationally, local Boxer units (called *t'uan* in rural areas and *t'an* in the cities) had from twenty-five to a hundred members and usually made their headquarters in the village temple. As might be expected of local peasant organizations, a wealth of superstition and supernaturalism was connected with the movement. Charms, incantations, and ritualized dancing, usually performed on the village "boxing ground," were thought to provide protection against injury and death in battle. The Boxers made much of the legends and myths of rural China, as well as poems and historical plays such as *Monkey, All Men Are Brothers,* and *The Romance of the Three Kingdoms.* A favorite hero was the famous medieval Chinese diplomat-leader Chu-ko-liang, whose trickery and astuteness had enchanted readers of *The Romance of the Three Kingdoms* for centuries.

Until the early months of 1899 the Boxer movement was simply an expression of local discontent in certain villages in Shantung Province and along the border between Shantung and Chihli. When antiforeign incidents had first erupted here in May 1898, the court had ordered the governors of the two provinces to investigate and take the necessary action. Governor Yü Lu of Chihli had suppressed the activity on the Chihli side of the border. Governor Chang Ju-mei of Shantung was not particularly sympathetic to the Boxer movement, but apparently he did not take it very seriously and was reluctant to use force to suppress it. In March 1899, however, Chang was replaced by Yü Hsien. Yü Hsien had been a judge in the administration of the anti-Western Li Ping-heng and was notoriously hostile to foreigners, particularly missionaries. With the province under his control, Boxer activities rapidly spread, and their actions became more violent.

Under the leadership of a peasant with the colorful pseudonym of Red Lantern Chu (Chu Hung-teng), the Boxers of Shantung began to loot and burn missionary compounds, railway stations, and the areas where Chinese Christian converts lived. When a local magistrate attempted to end riots at P'ing Yüan, killing a number of Boxers and dispersing the rest, Governor Yü Hsien angrily dismissed him. The message was loud and clear: the authorities, at least in Shantung Province, would condone anti-Western activities. A number of Boxer groups with several hundreds of members each, sensing official sympathy for their cause, began to circulate throughout Shantung Province, encountering no opposition from Governor Yü Hsien. In the opinion of many contemporary observers, Yü Hsien's dismissal of the magistrate marked the beginning of the Boxers' rise to national prominence.

In Peking the court vacillated between sympathy for the Boxers and reluctance to irritate the foreigners. When Chang Ju-mei, the moderate governor of Shantung Province who preceded Yü Hsien, had reported the rise of anti-foreign activities in his area, the Grand Council in Peking had ordered him to suppress the agitation. But by late 1899 the court had apparently developed a pro-Boxer position. It appeared anxious to turn the movement from an antidynastic to a prodynastic, anti-Western force. The court apparently even had some success in assimilating the Boxers into the local militia. As 1899 drew to a close, local Boxer groups began carrying four-character posters inscribed with the slogan, "Support the Ch'ing, Destroy the Foreigners."

When Yü Hsien removed the magistrate for suppressing Boxer riots at P'ing Yüan, Western diplomatic circles in Peking were outraged, and Edwin Conger, the American minister to China, demanded that the court dismiss Yü Hsien. In Conger's words, "If this governor will not or cannot control the rioters and protect these people, he should be removed at once and someone put in his place who can and will."[4] For a brief period the court resisted, but finally it acquiesced, and on December 6, 1899, Yü Hsien was recalled and replaced by Yüan Shih-k'ai. When Yüan left Hsiao Chan for Tsinan, the capital of Shantung Province, he took his Peiyang Army with him. Yüan, always the realist, was known to feel that the Boxers were a dangerous antidynastic movement which could easily turn against the court, and he was opposed to using a force which might unnecessarily incur foreign wrath against the Chinese government. On assuming his new duties, he quickly made it clear that, unlike his predecessor, he would not look benignly on Boxer activity in Shantung Province. Furthermore, he informed his subordinates that any local authorities permitting Boxer activities would be severely punished. He struck quickly at the rioters and executed Red Lantern Chu. When several Boxers volunteered to go before his firing squad to prove their invulnerability to bullets, he obliged. They were wrong.

Yüan Shih-k'ai's crackdown dramatically reduced the unrest in Shantung Province. It seemed clear that, although the court and the local authorities did not directly control the movement, official attitudes had much to do with the rise and decline of Boxer activities in north China. Yüan's own forceful repression of the Boxers did not totally end trouble in the region, however. Harassed by Yüan's forces, Boxer groups simply moved north into Chihli Province or into borderland areas where they could retreat to the opposite side when pursued by provincial military forces.

As the Boxers spread throughout the lowland areas near the capital, they evidently gained support from many elements in the local population, including the scholar-gentry, who began to view the movement as a righteous force cleansing China of its foreign enemies. Not all local officials sympathized with the movement, however. Magistrate Lao Nai-hsüan, author of the first serious study of the origins and nature of the movement, was convinced that the new prodynastic orientation of the Boxer leadership was a ruse and that the true nature of the movement was lawless and self-serving. As rioting increased in nearby districts in Chihli Province, Lao Nao-hsüan convened a meeting of his fellow magistrates in the vicinity and, with their concurrence, drew up a six-point program to suppress the movement. The program was sent to Governor Yü Lu, but he was apparently under pressure from antiforeign forces in nearby Peking and made no attempt to implement it.

In Peking the government was now clearly leaning toward the Boxers. Yü Hsien, who had been recalled from his post in Shantung "for an audience," found considerable support for his hard-line position at court. He was rewarded for his behavior in Shantung with the governorship of Shansi Province, a move that would have tragic consequences for hundreds of Christians in that area of north China. Acting Governor Yüan Shih-k'ai in Shantung was admonished by the court not to be too severe in his treatment of local Boxer groups and to make a careful distinction between loyalists and simple brigands.

By early spring of 1900 Boxer groups were moving north and west and were beginning to appear in the capital area. Youngsters were seen practicing Boxer drills within the city, and placards began to appear on city walls, predicting the burning of Peking and the destruction of the foreign legation quarters. The situation appeared even more ominous south of the capital along the Peking-Hankow railroad, where a number of missionary groups had extensive compounds. Roaming crowds of Boxers cut rail lines around the transportation hub of Pao Ting Fu and burned railway stations all along the line. More seriously, in Lai Shui district, they attacked an area inhabited by

Christian converts, killing sixty-eight and wounding many more. Boxers and government troops clashed in the area several times, but Governor Yü Lu, undoubtedly influenced by the situation at court, was reluctant to take strong action.

Opinion at the court in Peking was sharply divided. Moderates claimed that the Boxers were simply rebels who would harm China's relations with foreign powers and ultimately turn against the dynasty itself. If China cannot defeat Japan, they asked, how can it hope to defend itself against all the foreign powers at once? But the conservatives at court were becoming bold in expressing their resentment of Western activities. They tended to blame the foreigners, not only for the land-grab of 1898, but for K'ang Yu-wei's constitutional reform movement of the same year (K'ang had received considerable support from the British legation in Peking). Led by such Manchu nobles as K'ang Yi and Prince Tuan, the conservatives called for war and the destruction of the legations. Two middle-level officials presented to the court a proposal stating that there were only three options: to make peace; to abrogate the existing treaties and demand that the Westerners leave China; or to make war.

Throughout this frenzied period Tz'u Hsi kept her own counsel. Occasionally, she expressed exasperation at the Boxers, and one skeptic at court observed that they were "ripe for the cabbage market" (the site of executions in Peking). On the other hand, she apparently sincerely believed that the Boxers had magical powers, and moderates who dared to criticize them aroused her instant anger. A few moderates were executed, inspiring the reactionary Hsü T'ung to note with satisfaction, "The more of this kind of running dogs we kill the better." The militants were clearly in control, and China was moving inexorably toward war.

Chapter Four

The Escalating Crisis

The first mention of the Boxers by name, according to one student of the period, occurred in the *North China Daily News* on October 2, 1899. Until the first months of 1900, observers in world capitals and the legation quarter in Peking did not take the Boxers very seriously. Over the years the West had held a deep-rooted skepticism of the capacity of the Chinese to unite and resist the foreign challenge. Even by 1899, when the situation had grown serious, cries of alarm from missionaries in inland areas tended to be taken lightly by observers in Peking.

The legations, however, were capable of rapid action when trouble arose near the capital. In 1898, when the Muslim troops of General Tung Fu-hsiang had threatened Europeans in the Peking area, the ministers demanded that 130 European soldiers be dispatched to the capital to guard the foreign population. Despite official protests from the Chinese court, these troops remained in Peking until the following spring.

Incidents had been occurring sporadically in rural areas for years, but Western observers had received somewhat skeptically cries of alarm from the interior. Now, however, in the latter months of 1899 it appeared that the

45

new crisis would not simply go away. Reports from the outlying provinces increasingly expressed concern over the decline of social order and the rise of antiforeign sentiment among the Chinese population. Letters from missionaries described a serious situation—hostile crowds were harassing foreigners, chasing Chinese Christians from their villages and forcing them to barricade themselves in well-guarded "closed cities," and placards were appearing on foreigners' houses warning that their homes would be attacked and plundered.

At the end of the year a new development threatened to shatter the lingering complacency of the diplomatic corps in Peking. Evidence came to light that the Chinese court was strengthening its own determination to resist the tigerlike voracity of the imperialist powers. Chinese hostility had been escalating since the German takeover of Shantung in late 1897 and had been spurred by the fall of the reform party in Peking in late 1898. Firm action against Western demands had been prevented only by the strong pressure for compromise from moderates at court. But in 1899 the militant faction was solidifying its position at court, having gained confidence from its successful rebuff of the Italian demand for a naval base at San Men Bay. A secret decree sent to all viceroys, governors, and military commanders throughout the empire clearly expressed the change in attitude:

As the Italians have not had their ambitions gratified in respect to the cession of San Men Bay to them, it is apprehended that they may try to seek opportunity for seizing other portions of the coast. Moreover, the arbitrary and aggressive methods of the French at Kuang-chouwan, where they are stirring up disturbances in order to obtain pretexts for demanding concessions from the Imperial Government, may lead to actual hostilities between China and France. It behooves us, therefore, to exercise the utmost vigilance and watchfulness to guard against sudden aggression and to be always prepared to resist an enemy . . . . This yamen [court] has received the special commands of Her Imperial Majesty the Empress Dowager and His Imperial Majesty the Emperor to grant you full power and liberty to resist by force of arms all aggressions

The south wall of the Tartar city in Peking. The Chinese city is in the foreground. (*Leslie's Weekly*, July 14, 1900, cover)

upon your several jurisdictions, proclaiming a state of war, if necessary, without first asking for instructions from Peking, for this loss
of time may be fatal to your security and enable the enemy to make
good his footing against your forces.[1]

This secret edict came to the attention of the foreign
community in Peking at the end of the year, and on January
2 the text was transmitted by American Minister Conger to
Washington with the comment, "It would be a hopeful indication for the future of the Empire if China either could or
would carry it out, which is neither probable nor possible."
The disclosure of the new tough attitude of the
Chinese government was accompanied by further indications of the growing seriousness of the situation in the
countryside. On the last day of the year a British missionary, the Reverend S. M. Brooks, was brutally murdered by
a crowd of angry Chinese southwest of Tsinan. Evidently
the motive was revenge for the killing of a Chinese during
an earlier riot against missionaries. The slaying of Brooks
shocked the legations into realizing the seriousness of the
crisis. Sir Claude MacDonald, British minister in Peking
and *doyen* of all the diplomatic representatives in China,
immediately complained to the Tsungli Yamen, the
Chinese Ministry of Foreign Affairs, and demanded that
the perpetrators be punished. On January 4 the court
issued a decree which appeared to meet MacDonald's
demands. It called for the punishment of those responsible
for Brooks's death and of those local Chinese officials
whose negligence had permitted the incident to occur. A
week later, however, a second decree was published which
renewed concern in the legation quarter. It stated that
those "bad characters and rebels" who "form themselves
into bands" to plunder and riot would be ruthlessly
suppressed by the government; on the other hand, "if
law-abiding people and loyal people combine to drill for
their own protection, or villages join for mutual defense,
this is only to fulfill the subject's duty of keeping watch
and ward."[2] The court was clearly instructing local gov-

ernments to differentiate between patriotic and lawless elements. To the ministers in Peking, the January 11 decree had an ominous ring. French minister Stéphen Pichon called it "vague and elastic," and Conger said that he had "some anxiety as to the effect of its strange wording."

It was clear that the dynasty was still vacillating between considering the Boxers antidynastic troublemakers and treating them as patriots who would aid the throne in its hour of need. The distinctions made in the second decree accurately reflected the growing division at court. Tension marked the relationship between Jung Lu, a moderate confidant of the empress dowager and commander of the imperial forces around the capital, and Prince Tuan, the reactionary xenophobe described by Conger as "malignantly antiforeign."

Further evidence indicated that the hard-liners were becoming the dominant figures at court. After Prince Tuan had his son P'u Chün declared heir to the throne (on the grounds that Kuang Hsü's "illness" prevented him from producing an heir), a purge of moderates took place and Weng T'ung-ho, the prominent imperial tutor to Kuang Hsü, was among those arrested. A few days later Yü Hsien, only recently dismissed from his gubernatorial post due to legation protests, was appointed governor of Shansi Province. Yü Hsien had spent the period since his dismissal in Peking, and presumably his influence had helped tip the scales in favor of the militants.

The legations felt that it was necessary to voice their displeasure with the court's ambivalence. On January 27, at the behest of French Minister Pichon, the ministers of Britain, Germany, France, and the United States submitted a joint note to the Tsungli Yamen in which they protested the equivocal nature of the January 11 decree and demanded that another decree be issued prohibiting further antiforeign activities and dissolving the Boxer movement. For several weeks the court did not deign to reply.

It quickly became apparent that the decrees emanating

from the palace were not lessening the violence in the countryside. The Boxers, driven from Shantung into Chihli Province by Yüan Shih-k'ai's energetic activities, were filtering into the capital and the foreign concession area at Tientsin. In diplomatic circles worrisome rumors spread that the eight thousand troops of Kansu general Tung Fu-hsiang, camped just outside the capital walls, were preparing to join the Boxers.

The ministers were thoroughly alarmed at the continuing crisis and correctly surmised that antiforeign elements were reading between the lines of the imperial decrees to discern official sympathy for their activities. Consequently, they sent a second note to the Tsungli Yamen, reiterating their demands of January 27 and further demanding that a new decree, explicitly prohibiting Boxer activities, be published in the *Peking Gazette,* the official publication of the government. The Chinese refused, contending that such a decree was unsuitable for publication in the *Gazette.* On March 10 the ministers returned to the attack, claiming in a joint note that, if their demands were refused, they would inform their governments and ask them to take "the proper means" to "guarantee the security of our nationals." As an additional step, the legations suggested to their home governments that they consider staging a naval demonstration in the coastal waters of north China if the situation did not immediately improve.

IMPERIALIST RIVALRY

As antiforeign sentiment in Peking increased unchecked and the powers were gradually compelled to consider concerted political or even military initiatives, the inherent diversity of the motives and goals of the foreign powers in China began to grow more obvious. Even as the crisis in north China intensified, the imperialist powers found themselves more anxious over the activities of their rivals than over those of the Chinese themselves.

France's main rival was Great Britain; the two nations had been in competition for the China market since mid-century. Concern over the British occupation of Burma had led the French into Indochina as a means of seeking a southern entry into the Chinese heartland. Later, to counter the British advance in the central and lower Yangtse Valley, the French had attempted to carve out a sphere of influence in the Chinese provinces along the southern border. While the animosity between the two countries had diminished somewhat by the end of the century, it was still sufficiently strong to animate suspicion among diplomats in the two countries. As the crisis in China grew, the French minister in Peking, Stéphen Pichon, as well as French diplomatic and consular officials elsewhere in China, continually voiced their concern at the nefarious activities of their British counterparts. They believed that the British wanted to divide China and establish a dominant position in the central Yangtse provinces, and, if this were the case, France was determined not to be left out.[3]

Though suspicious of each other, France and Britain did have mutual interests in China. Neither felt that anything could be gained from the dismemberment of the Chinese empire, and, as the crisis developed, each was prepared to join with the other in an attempt to maintain China's territorial integrity. For the British, the greatest threat to that territorial integrity, as well as to their own areas of influence in East Asia, came not from France, but from Russia. The newly active Germans, obstreperous and sometimes heavy-handed, seemed likely to cause trouble for all powers with interests in the China market. Germany, though, was hardly a threat to Great Britain's dominant position in China. Russia was another matter. For years British observers had suspected that the Russians intended to become the dominant power throughout all of north China, and they were not far wrong. Russian influence in East Asia had been stimulated by the territorial gains achieved after the wars of 1858-1860. By the end of the century the Russians were advancing gradually but persistently, not only into Outer Mongolia and Chinese Turkestan, but also in the area northeast of the Great Wall. They had negotiated an agreement with Peking to build a rail line directly across the heart of Manchuria to the port of Vladivostok on the Pacific coast. In 1900 St. Petersburg did not have any immediate aims for further territorial expansion in the area. Russia was content to assimilate its new sphere of influence in the Liaotung Peninsula and to develop commercial activities throughout the three provinces of Manchuria. But Russia's long-term plans, epitomized by the far-seeing strategy of Minister of Finance Count Witte, included a desire to bring all of north China under full Russian domination.

In their concern over Russian advances in East Asia, the British had a potential ally in Japan, who, having recently strengthened its position in Korea in the war of 1894-1895, was determined to forestall possible Russian expansion in southern Manchuria and in the Korean peninsula, an expansion that was already well underway.

If the British were concerned at Russian successes in the north, the latter returned the hostility in full measure. To St. Petersburg, Russian advances in Asia were simply a process of manifest destiny, an extension of the Russian empire's centuries-old eastward expansion beyond the Urals and across the frozen wastes of Siberia. Since the middle of the nineteenth century Russia's greatest rival in this process had been Great Britain. London had countered Russian advances east of the Caspian Sea by moving into Afghanistan and had reacted to growing Russian influence in Turkestan by attempting to solidify a position in isolated Tibet. The Boxer crisis simply added a new dimension to the worldwide Russo-British rivalry.

The Russians felt that it was unfair to portray their policy toward China in purely selfish terms. In the view of the tsarist court, Russia was the only true friend of China among the European powers. Convinced that its geographical position carried with it a unique sympathy for the needs and aspirations of the Chinese, the government at St. Petersburg saw itself as the true protector of the Chinese against the rapacity of the other imperialist powers. In 1860 Russia had stepped in to mediate a settlement at the end of the Lorcha Arrow Wars (and in the process had managed to detach several thousand square miles of Chinese territory as compensation) and in 1896 had signed a secret treaty of friendship with Peking in conjunction with the agreement permitting Russia to build railroads in Manchuria. As the Boxer crisis developed, Russian policy was persistently distinguished by ambivalence—a wish to help Peking against the other powers, and a desire to profit from China's troubles by solidifying Russian influence in north China.

The United States, the other major power in China, also took an ambivalent position toward the court's reaction to the Boxers. It had participated in the commercial and missionary activities in China during the previous half century and had a general concern for the interests and safety of American residents there. Its commercial interests in particular had increased rapidly during the 1890s, and the United States was on the verge of developing major economic and political needs in the Western Pacific. Yet America's long-standing anticolonial tradition and its lingering distrust of alliances with other powers had led it to a deliberately independent position in China as the crisis deepened. Maintaining a balance between isolation and collaboration with the other Westerners in China would prove to be increasingly difficult. The suspicion in world capitals regarding the court's intentions was reflected in the diplomatic community in Peking. As might be expected in the case of a small and virtually self-contained community, the personalities of the ministers themselves frequently came into play. The *dramatis personae* in Peking were an interesting lot, but their diverse characteristics led to misunderstanding and a mutual lack of respect which would result in considerable difficulty as the crisis unfolded.[4]

Sir Claude MacDonald, the
British minister in Peking
(*Leslie's Weekly*, August 18,
1900, p. 119)

Edwin Conger, the American
minister in Peking (*Leslie's
Weekly*, July 28, 1900, p.64)

Stephen Pichon, the French
minister in Peking (*Leslie's
Weekly*, July 28, 1900, p.64)

Baron Klemens von Ketteler,
the German minister in Peking
(*Leslie's Weekly* July 28, 1900,
p. 64)

British Minister Sir Claude MacDonald was the acknowledged head of the diplomatic community in Peking. An ex-military officer with the Scot's Greys, MacDonald was a steady but unspectacular performer who had not earned high plaudits during the early years of his tour in Peking. The German minister, Baron Klemens von Ketteler, was almost his direct opposite. Like MacDonald, he had a military background, having served in Peking as military attaché during the 1880s. This assignment had gained him a reputation as one of the few "China hands" among the foreign ministers in Peking. Von Ketteler, who allegedly possessed in generous measure the arrogance often associated with Prussian aristocrats, was as flamboyant as MacDonald was stolid, and, although he was married to an attractive American wife, rumors circulated that he was involved in several love affairs in the Peking diplomatic community.

Stephen Pichon, MacDonald's counterpart in the French legation, possessed a generous sense of *amour-propre* and a lively suspicion of all his colleagues. In his dispatches (now available at the Quai d'Orsay in Paris) Pichon emerges as somewhat pompous and petty. Unlike most of his colleagues, he began to voice his concern about the Boxers when most foreigners were inclined to scoff at the danger. Pichon's persistent references to the activities of "les Boxeurs" caused considerable merriment within the diplomatic community until reports from the countryside began to prove that his warnings were not exaggerated. Pichon had an advantage over his colleagues. He was receiving periodic reports on Boxer activities in the provinces from the French bishop of Peking, Monsignor Favier, who in turn received appeals for help from French missionaries scattered throughout China.

The Russian minister was the fairly colorless M. N. de Giers. Edwin Conger, the representative from the United States, was a political appointee from the Midwest with little experience in foreign affairs. A commoner in an aristocratic profession and an amateur at the art of diplomacy, Conger was generally considered a lightweight in the councils of the ministers in Peking. Moreover, there are indications that his own superior, Secretary John Hay, had serious reservations about his capabilities.

The call by the ministers for naval demonstrations in the waters off north China did not meet with strong support from most of the home governments. In London, Foreign Secretary Salisbury was reluctant to take such a drastic step, considering it "not without danger" and premature under the circumstances. Lord Salisbury's attitude reflected a trend in British policy toward caution and against active involvement in Chinese affairs. Washington evinced a similar attitude. Although Conger in Peking had endorsed the request, Secretary Hay refused to participate and informed the British ambassador that Washington did not feel it could join in a naval demonstration which it felt was "contrary to its traditions." Actually, Hay was feeling his way cautiously in the crisis. As he later conceded to a friend, he had been badly informed on the situation and was anxious to avoid taking a provocative stand, since imperialism and executive authority were likely to be major issues in the upcoming presidential campaign. To protect his diplomatic flank, he telegraphed Conger on June 10 instructing him:

We have no policy in China except to protect with energy American interests, and especially American citizens and the legation. There must be nothing done which would commit us to future action inconsistent with your standing instructions. There must be no alliances[5]

Domestically, the purpose of the telegram was obvious since it was immediately given out to the press.

The French, too, felt that a naval demonstration was premature and decided to hold off temporarily, but the Ministry of the Marine was instructed to hold the Pacific Fleet in readiness. The Russians, with only two hundred and fifty citizens residing in China, also wanted to maintain an independent position and refused to get involved in a possible joint action. The Germans were less reluctant, and Berlin proceeded to dispatch warships to Chinese coastal waters. In response, Salisbury ordered two British ships to the area, "a simple measure of precaution," he said, "destined to satisfy English citizens and to awaken the government of China to the perils of a policy of hostility with regard to strangers." Washington, while still denying the need for a joint naval demonstration, also reacted to Berlin's move, and at the end of March ordered an American vessel, the *Wheeler,* to proceed from Manila Bay to the waters off north China. Secretary Hay was obviously nervous and told French Minister Jules Cambon that he believed Minister Conger in Peking to be "excessively zealous." If Conger threatened the Chinese with landing American military troops, said the secretary, he would be disavowed in Washington.

THE GROWING CRISIS

For a brief period it looked as though the situation in China might improve. In early April, with the Boxers increasing their activities in Chihli Province and rapidly approaching the capital, the Tsungli Yamen published in the *Peking Gazette* a report by Viceroy Yü Lu of Chihli containing the text of the decree that the ministers had earlier demanded be published. In response to this apparent about-face in the official attitude toward the Boxers, Chihli officials were temporarily inclined to put down disorder with severity. The shift in attitude, however, was more apparent than real. By late April Boxer groups were congregating along the north-south Peking-Hankow railway line, and on April 24 two thousand Boxers attacked a Catholic village at Chiang Chia Chuang near the rail hub of Pao Ting Fu. The Chinese Christians in the area had been prepared for the attack and defended themselves with courage. As a result, the Boxer forces were defeated and the defenders suffered only light losses. Elsewhere, however, Boxers began to appear openly in the Chinese sections of Peking and Tientsin, and anxiety increased in the legation quarter. Besieged by appeals from French missionary groups in Chihli Province, Minister Pichon began pressing his colleagues for energetic action to compel the court to maintain order. For a time, Conger and MacDonald refrained from putting pressure on the Chinese, fearing that to do so might lead to a collapse of the government and the onset of anarchy.

By late May, however, it became clear that Pichon's warnings had to be taken seriously. The news of the attack on the Chinese Christian village south of Pao Ting Fu was supplemented by rumors of an impending massacre of all foreigners in China. Early in May Pichon received an urgent message from the doughty bishop of Peking, Monsignor Favier, reporting that sixty of his Chinese converts had been burned alive during a Boxer attack. Rumors circulated that the Boxers were surrounding the capital and lighting fires in the heart of Peking. Placards appeared announcing the imminent annihilation of missionaries and a general uprising against all foreigners. Favier relayed a report received from an informant that the Boxers planned to enter Peking *en masse* at a signal, and added that he needed a minimum of forty to fifty French sailors to protect the Peitang Catholic Cathedral in the heart of the city. On May 20 the ministers accepted Pichon's proposal to send a message to the Tsungli Yamen demanding that the government take immediate measures to restore secure conditions. The ministers unanimously agreed that, if the situation did not improve, they would formally request a naval demonstration and the dispatch of troops from the ships stationed off the coastal waters near Taku. In response to appeals for help from citizens in the provinces, they advised all missionaries living in outlying areas to send their dependents to more secure areas in the center, where they were considered safe under the protection of viceroys Chang Chih-tung and Liu K'un-yi.

Official Chinese opinion continued to vacillate. In the first few days of May the court discussed the possibility of assimilating the Boxer groups into the militia and asked Yü Lu and Yüan Shih-k'ai to concur. By May 16 both governors had responded in the negative. Yü Lu's reply was to the point. He said that most Boxers were only roving troublemakers who tried to seduce the people and make private profit. As a rule, they lacked military talent, and it would be difficult to assimilate and control them. For the moment the court withheld action on the matter.

As massacres of Christians continued during the final days of May, and the Tsungli Yamen resisted giving total satisfaction, the powers began to consider further action. Pichon called the French ship *Descartes* to Shantung, and the Russians ordered two ships from Port Arthur. These measures did nothing to alleviate the crisis. On May 28 the legations received news of further attacks by Boxer units at Pao Ting Fu — railway stations and bridges had been burned and a number of foreigners killed. The survivors, mostly railroad engineers and their families, had managed to escape on foot and fled toward the foreign concession area at Tientsin. Several were killed en route in scattered Boxer attacks; the remainder were rescued by a troop of Russian Cossacks sent from Tientsin.

Reports of the attacks at Pao Ting Fu galvanized the legations into action. The ministers decided unanimously to request a call-up of military forces from the warships off the coast near Taku. The Tsungli Yamen was informed of the decision and asked to make trains ready at Taku to bring the foreign troops to the capital. The court, apparently warned that open confrontation with the foreigners might occur, immediately responded that it was taking action and asked the ministers to postpone their decision. At the same time it issued a decree calling on local authorities to arrest Boxer leaders and disperse their followers. As before, the decree drew a delicate distinction between vagabonds and troublemakers and loyal elements. The ambiguity was sufficient to negate at the local level the potential effects of the decree on behalf of the foreigners.

The ministers refused the request of the Tsungli

Yamen to postpone this call-up of forces. Indeed, Pichon had already instructed French forces to get underway, and British Minister MacDonald informed the Tsungli Yamen that troops would be sent, with or without Chinese permission. If transport was not provided by the government, the joint force would be sent on foot and come in augmented numbers. On May 31 the resistance of the Chinese government collapsed, and the foreigners were given permission to move their troops, provided the number of guards was limited to no more than thirty for each legation. The decision had not been an easy one for the court to make, and, according to one student of the period, it was the troop call-up that precipitated the eventual outbreak of conflict. There was serious discussion within the court of the possibility of stopping the Western troops by force. K'ang Yi, one of the more determined members of the antiforeign faction, proposed to resist them at the gates of Peking. The moderates, led by Jung Lu and Prince Ch'ing, were able to reject the suggestion only with considerable difficulty.

On May 30 Russian and French troops had begun to leave their ships off the coast at Taku. Chinese troops in the vicinity menaced them and threatened to fire, so they immediately reembarked and waited for further instructions. After permission had been received from Peking on May 31, debarkation resumed. The contingent sent to Peking consisted of 340 men — 75 Russians, 75 British, 75 French, 50 Americans, 40 Italians, and 25 Japanese. Despite the Chinese stipulation that only 30 men per country be deployed, they met no opposition and arrived at the capital in the early morning of June 2. An additional contingent of 52 Germans and 37 Austrians followed soon afterward. The majority of the troops available to the powers remained on shipboard off the coast.

The dispatch of the legation guards from Taku to the capital exacerbated the crisis at court. Moderates such as Jung Lu wanted the Boxers suppressed. Although not particularly motivated by sympathy for the foreigners, they were convinced that war with the barbarians would lead to disaster for China. Although they were able to win approval for the troop movement, they were over-ruled on other issues by the war party. At one meeting, when the militants argued that the Boxers were patriots and should be treated as supporters of the dynasty, the empress dowager significantly kept silent.

The actions of the court were more eloquent than words. When forces under General Nieh Shih-ch'eng clashed with Boxers who had burned railway stations on the Tientsin-Peking line and killed hundreds of innocent Chinese, he was reproved by the court. It was evident that the empress dowager was leaning toward the reactionaries. On June 6 the Grand Council made a half-hearted decision to disband the Boxers, but a mission sent by the court to see the Boxer leaders near Peking failed to achieve results. The members of the mission were unable to see the rebel leaders and, according to one account, simply posted proclamations in the Boxer camp. However, they returned to the capital, with demands from the Boxer leaders: withdraw the military troops of Nieh Shih-ch'eng from the vicinity of the capital; punish all magistrates who had taken hostile actions against Boxer elements; and permit the Moslem troops under General Tung Fu-hsiang to attack the foreigners. The third suggestion was rejected, but the first two were soon to be implemented. Once again, the court issued a decree which drew a distinction between the Boxers, who were considered to have formed legitimately for "self-defense purposes," and bandits who were interested simply in stirring up social disorder. Significantly, the decree was also critical of "bad elements" within the Chinese Christian community. The Chinese court was moving inexorably closer to a confrontation with the foreigners.[6]

The strengthening of the antiforeign attitude at court, combined with the growing boldness of Boxer attacks in Chihli Province, worried the legations. On June 6 rioters cut the rail links between the capital and Tientsin, halfway to the coast. The ministers, facing the possibility of complete isolation in Peking, sent a joint telegram asking their governments to instruct the naval authorities at Taku "to take concerted measures for our relief." Some proposed even harsher measures. The German minister, Baron von Ketteler, wanted to march on the summer palace and overthrow the empress dowager.

Reaction in world capitals to the new developments in China was mixed. British Foreign Secretary Salisbury was inclined to trust his man-on-the-spot and informed MacDonald and Admiral Edward Seymour, British naval commander at Taku, to take whatever action they deemed necessary. Several British warships—the *Centurion,* the *Endymion,* the *Whiting,* and the *Fame*—had just arrived off Taku to strengthen Seymour's flotilla. The French government decided to dispatch a fleet of ships to China under Admiral Cournejelles to be held at Minister Pichon's disposition. The Russian admiral at Port Arthur declared himself ready to send five thousand Russian troops if needed, and Minister Giers in Peking was authorized by St. Petersburg to call on these forces if he deemed it necessary.

Washington continued to hold back, however, despite Conger's plea for joint action. Secretary Hay feared that the United States would be drawn into an anti-Chinese alliance. He told the French ambassador in Washington that American actions in China would necessarily be limited, since the nation's forces in Asia were currently being used to suppress the guerrilla insurrection led by nationalist general Aguinaldo in the Philippines. Hay did agree to dispatch a token force of marines whose duties would be limited to protecting the American legation. They would not be permitted, he said, to join in a collective action against China.

Despite Hay's position, there were signs that the United States was being gradually drawn into an anti-Chinese coalition. Certain representatives of the American press were incensed at Boxer attacks on Christian missionaries and called on the McKinley administration to show some backbone in protecting American and Christian interests in China. The French ambassador to Washington, Jules Cambon, noted that the United States, "which had always affected not to talk of Chinese affairs," had "suddenly changed its attitude." Possibly as a trial balloon, a dispatch by Minister Conger describing the alarming situation in north China was given to the press, along with a report by Admiral Louis Kempff, commander of American forces at Taku.

Hay sent ambiguous instructions to his minister in Peking, advising him to "act independently in protection of American interests where practicable, and concurrently with representatives of other powers if necessity arise." Hay was obviously in a difficult position. He explained to the French ambassador that the American troops already in China were there only to protect the American legation, but when Cambon pressed him on American actions in the event of war, he agreed that it might be necessary to place American forces in China under joint allied command. As Hay explained the situation, the United States would agree to "concordance" but not "accord" with the actions of the powers. Presumably, the secretary was attempting to distinguish between informal cooperation and formal agreement. This subtle distinction would prove difficult, if not impossible, to maintain in practice.

Within China the situation was rapidly deteriorating. On June 4 the telegraph lines from Peking were cut. Except for the imperial telegraph line, all telecommunications with the coast were severed. Two days later news arrived that the Boxers intended to burn the Peitang cathedral, which was promptly placed under guard. On June 7 the Boxers set fire to the thatch roof of a police hut adjacent to the legation quarter; European volunteers from a neighboring building put out the blaze while the police at the post apparently still slept inside the hut. Word then began circulating that the Boxers intended to burn not only the legation quarter, but also the nearby Tsungli Yamen, the symbol of China's humiliation at the hands of the West. When he heard of the plan, British Minister MacDonald was prompted to comment with some irony, "In that case I hope a favorable wind will carry the fire toward the palace." On June 8 Russian Orthodox missions just outside the walls of the city were burned. On the following day, as usual, the train left Machiapu, at the south entrance to the capital, for the coast. Because of Boxer attacks in the area to the east of Peking, it would be the last train to leave the capital for the sea until the end of the crisis.

The diplomatic corps promptly asked the Chinese government for permission to request additional troops, but the request was refused. At court antiforeign elements were now in complete command. Ominously, a shift of personnel took place at the Tsungli Yamen which, under the presidency of Prince Ch'ing had long been a source of moderate attitudes within the Chinese government. On June 9 Prince Ch'ing was replaced by Prince Tuan, a die-hard of the antiforeign bloc. Three other Manchu reactionaries—Ch'i Hsiu, Na T'ung, and P'u Hsing—were also appointed to the group. For the first time the Tsungli Yamen became an instrument of the pro-war faction. Minister Conger, on hearing the news, called these appointments "extremely unfortunate" for the safety of the foreigners in Peking.

The menacing situation around Peking soon—and perhaps inevitably—erupted into violence. Until now foreign residents in Peking had not been personally harassed or threatened. On June 9, however, a contingent of Boxers burned the grandstand at the International Race Course just beyond the south gates of the city. Incinerated in the conflagration were a number of Chinese Christian converts who had apparently been brought there expressly for that purpose. A group of young British diplomats out for a ride on horseback came upon the scene by accident and had to flee for their lives.

This incident prompted British Minister MacDonald,

on his own initiative, to send a telegram to Admiral Seymour:

Situation extremely grave, unless arrangements are made for immediate advance to Peking it will be too late.

(At the time someone unkindly remarked that MacDonald was more worried about his horses than about the human lives involved.) Then on June 10 the summer homes of several British legation families, located on a hill to the west of Peking, were looted and burned. Only with difficulty were the British dependents — women and children — rescued and brought to the legation quarter. The next day the chancellor of the Japanese legation, Akira Sugiyama, left the quarter to find out whether additional detachments of foreign troops had arrived. Nearing the Yung Ting gate, he was murdered by some of the Kansu troops of General Tung Fu-hsiang. Sugiyama was the first member of the legation staffs to be harmed by the antiforeign element. The murder was a harsh demonstration that the diplomatic corps was not exempt from attack.

The crisis seemed to intensify daily. On June 11 the telegraph line to Russia (through Kalgan and Kiakhta), the last tie to Europe, was severed (although it was briefly re-established the next day, it was permanently cut on the thirteenth). By that evening, the entire area to the northeast of the legation quarter in Peking was in flames, including several Western missions and churches. With Boxer attacks rapidly approaching the very doorstep of the legation quarter, the people inside were finally persuaded to try to protect themselves. On June 13 Boxers began to enter the quarter, and the ministers took their first actions to isolate themselves from the contagion in the city. That afternoon temporary barricades were erected at both ends of Legation Street and at the northern and southern termini of Customs Street on the eastern border of the quarter. Patrols were set up in the area to drive Boxers

from the streets and to shoot those who appeared. Foreigners and Chinese Christians living in the city who could
not find protection elsewhere began gathering in the legation quarter, Favier's Peitang Cathedral, the Nan T'ang
Cathedral in the Chinese city, and at the American
Methodist Mission to the east. At the mission several hundred converts were guarded by a small contingent of U.S.
Marines. At the Peitang Cathedral Favier called urgently
for assistance, and a party of forty-three French and
Italian marines was dispatched in response.

Obviously, the Boxers had become a serious threat.
That evening large crowds of Boxers gathered at the
Imperial Bank just east of the quarter on Ch'ang An
Street. Attempting to set fire to the bank, they were
driven back by Austrian troops nearby, but they soon
turned on the foreign defenses. A foreign member of the
Imperial Maritime Customs in the area at the time des-
cribed the sight:

Everything had been quiet after the first ten minutes, when a few
volleys scattered the half-hearted Boxers, who had attempted to set
fire to the Imperial Bank of China (so ardent is the patriotism of
these Boxers that they destroy indiscriminately Government railways and the Government banks!), but about 10:30 lights were seen
approaching.
　　These increased in number, and soon the Austrians felt sure that
a mob of several thousands was approaching with torches to fire
their Legation and the Customs. They waited until the lights came
within a hundred yards, and then bang, bang, bang went their guns,
and volley after volley rang out, and it seemed that nothing could
live under that hail of bullets . . . . At the first volley the centre of
the line of torches was simply wiped out, and after the fourth there
were only a few lights to be seen. But what I can't understand is that
not one sound, not one moan, was heard.[7]

That same night the Boxers attacked and set fire to
the Nan T'ang Cathedral, built in 1622. Trapped inside and
burned to death were several hundred Chinese Christians,
inhabitants of the area who had sought safety in the
cathedral. A patrol sent out from the legation quarter ar-

rived too late. They found the church in ashes and several hundred corpses smoldering in the ruins.

The following few days saw a continuation of the violence. On the night of the fourteenth all foreign premises outside of the guarded area were burned, including fifty-four Protestant dwellings, eighteen chapels, twenty-seven schools, and nineteen dispensaries and hospitals. Not all the destruction was aimed specifically at the foreigner. On the evening of June 16 Boxers set fire to several shops which catered to foreigners in the commercial sector of the Chinese city, not far from the south wall. According to Richard O'Connor, author of *The Spirit Soldiers: A Narrative of the Boxer Rebellion,* the Boxer leader responsible had intended to destroy only certain selected shops and had believed that his magical powers would prevent the spread of the conflagration. He had overestimated the force of his persuasions, however, and before the fire burned out, it had destroyed several blocks of shops as well as the tower of the famous Ch'ien Men, the imperial entrance along the south wall of the Tartar city.[8]

As the situation rapidly deteriorated, the legations attempted to strike back. Troop patrols were sent out on actual raids; on June 16 one group located over fifty Boxers looting a Chinese temple and killed them all in cold blood. Some of the legation troops at the barricades began to fire at the soldiers of Tung Fu-hsiang's army, who by this time had joined the Boxers in the growing siege surrounding the quarter.

Similar conditions existed in Tientsin. On June 2 Boxers raced through the foreign concession area setting buildings afire. On the fourteenth Boxer elements entered the native city in force, evoking no response from the local administration. More buildings were burned in the foreign concession area, and mobs destroyed chapels and the famous French Catholic Cathedral in the heart of the city.

During this week of semi-siege, Boxers circulated freely throughout both cities but made no concentrated attacks on foreign-held areas. They seemed to be waiting for a word from authority. As for the Chinese government, it seemed to be either powerless or unwilling to take any action to quiet the situation. It was clear to all that the worst was yet to come. The attacks had shown the foreigners a side of the Chinese temperament that they had not known existed. One foreign observer described an exchange of fire with Boxer groups near the legation quarter:

An hour afterwards we heard the most terrible and awful sound that we had ever imagined. The sky was rent with yells of "Sha, sha" [kill, kill], and the whole city seemed to be battering at the gates and thirsting for our blood. It was the yell of wild beasts; no pen could describe it; and our blood simply froze in our veins.

It was not the fear of what they could do—most of them, in fact, almost all, were only armed with swords; but it was our first dreadful peep into the depths of a Chinaman's heart, and we saw there the deadly, undying wild beast hate of the foreigner that we had barely guessed at before.[9]

Chapter Five

The International
Detachments

O n the evening of June 9 Admiral Edward
Seymour, commander of the British naval forces
in north China waters and the senior officer
among the allied commanders in the area, received a telegram from Sir Claude MacDonald asking
urgently for assistance. Seymour immediately wired back
that a relief force under his command was just leaving the
coast and heading for Peking. Seymour's reply was the last
message received by the legations before all communication with the outside world was cut off.

MacDonald had sent his hasty telegram after the
burning of the Peking International Race Course, and the
wire had finally spurred to action the military forces off
the north China coast. The decision to act had not been
easy for the Western military commanders. Warships had
been congregating off the China coast at the port city of
Taku since late in May. By early June fifteen warships of
various nationalities were already anchored near the mouth
of the Pei Ho, and more were expected shortly. Through
communications from the legation quarter in Peking the

allied commanders were aware that the situation in north China had become critical, but they had not received specific orders from their home governments. In the absence of such instructions they had the power to take such actions as they saw fit to protect the lives and property of their nationals in China.

The original contingent of guards had been sent to Peking by rail on May 31 in response to the request of the legations. On June 4, after hearing of the attacks at Pao Ting Fu and the murder of several Europeans by marauding bands of Boxers, the commanders sent an additional mixed force by rail to the capital. The next day Admiral Seymour called a joint conference to arrange for coordinated action among the powers in case hostilities broke out. At a subsequent meeting it was agreed that, if the legations were physically cut off from communication with the coast, the commanders would dispatch a relief force to Peking.

On receiving MacDonald's urgent appeal on June 9, Seymour acted quickly. He immediately ordered the debarkation of troops from British warships off Taku and at six o'clock the following morning left with them by train for Tientsin, some thirty miles inland. Seymour's action was considered by some to be unduly precipitous, especially since he had not informed the other allied commanders personally of his decision. Instead, he left messages suggesting that they follow his action at their earliest opportunity. Seymour's troops arrived in Tientsin after an uneventful trip. By the end of the day most of the other Western commanders had followed his lead, and a relief force of about two thousand men of various nationalities (915 British, 450 Germans, 358 French, 312 Russians, 112 Americans, 54 Japanese, 40 Italians, and 25 Austrians) had gathered for an advance to Peking.

At the time Seymour's apparent aim was to transport his troops all the way to Peking by rail. Since much of the Tientsin-Peking line had been destroyed by Boxer attacks, he planned to take with him material for repairs along the way. On his arrival at Tientsin Seymour had requested per-

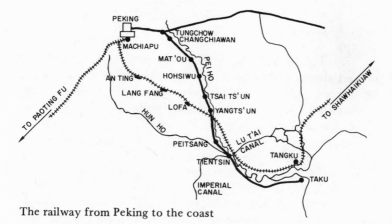

The railway from Peking to the coast

mission from local authorities to requisition railroad cars to transport his troops to Peking. Governor-General Yü Lu was somewhat reluctant, but at 9:30 A.M. on June 11 he gave his permission. The relief force of slightly over two thousand men, with three days' provisions, left immediately for Peking. Seymour hoped to arrive at the capital later the same day. But between Tientsin and Peking were uncounted numbers of Boxers and the imperial military forces of Nieh Shih-ch'eng.

With the approach of Admiral Seymour's mixed force, the Chinese government faced a crucial question. Did tne Chinese army have the ability to protect the capital and resist the Western forces? Since the middle of the nineteenth century periodic military confrontations with Western powers had consistently resulted in defeat and humiliation. In fact, the main cause for China's failure to stem Western aggression was the poor quality of its military forces. Under the Manchus, the Chinese army had traditionally been divided into two main forces—the Manchu bannermen, two hundred thousand strong, and the so-called Green Standard Army, a force of five hundred thousand native Chinese troops under Chinese command. The Green Standard forces were poorly trained and had proven useless in combat. Their officers regularly claimed to have more men under their command than actually existed in order to claim their salaries, and were generally corrupt.

During the Taiping rebellion at midcentury, the hard-pressed dynasty had been unable to resist the rebels with the forces under central command. Thus, it had been compelled to agree to the establishment of local forces which would defend the provinces and fight the rebels. In the aftermath of the rebellion these provincial forces had grown into cumbersome armies under the control of governors and viceroys and were totally divorced from the control of central authorities.

In the last decade of the nineteenth century the court began to make some halting efforts to reform the Chinese military establishment, particularly after the defeat by Japan.[1] A few progressive officials had suggested that the province-based Green Standard armies be disbanded and replaced by new modern armies of several hundred thousand well-trained troops. Others advocated the establishment of modern military schools, the hiring of foreign military advisers, and a complete reorganization of the empire's entire defense system. In the waning years of the century a few attempts were made by the dynasty to implement these suggestions. Foreign officers were hired to provide modern training in weapons and tactics, arsenals were built, and a few modern weapons were purchased. Most important, two modern armies were organized and put under the command of two of the more influential Chinese civil officials in the empire. The so-called Self-strengthening Army of Chang Chih-tung, viceroy of Wuchang, was established in the central provinces of the Yangtse Valley. The second was the New, or Peiyang, Army, set up by Yüan Shih-k'ai in the northern area near the capital. These two forces were to be formulated along Western lines, with separate units for infantry, cavalry, and artillery. They were to be armed with modern weapons and trained by foreign advisers. The two armies were to form the nucleus of a modernized defense force that could

protect China against outside attack. Both Chang and
Yüan believed that the key to an efficient army was the
quality of the officers and men. Their officers were to be
well trained and incorruptible, the troops literate and well
paid. With support from central revenues, the new modern
armies were able to recruit the best among the Green
Standard Army, and both forces totaled several thousand
men as the century came to a close.

The reform of China's outmoded defense establishment would require a lot more than two crack modern
armies. The entire system was corrupt, the soldier was held
in low esteem in Chinese society, and there were no
modern weapons or training personnel. Finally, there was
no central control over the remaining Green Standard
forces. These factors combined to make the modernization
of China's armies almost impossible.

In 1898, desperate to find a means of resisting the
encroachments of Western powers, the court agreed to
a plan calling for the formation of a Chinese militia. The
idea had originally been proposed by K'ang Yu-wei and implemented during the hundred days of reform in the summer of 1898. When Tz'u Hsi was restored to power in
September, she agreed to continue with the plan. The
function of the proposed militia was not clear; according
to one source, they were to be used internally for protection against bandits. Their training and weaponry would
almost certainly prove inadequate for combat against
foreigners. These vague aspects of the militia plan created
confusion in the minds of foreign observers, and some
contended that the militia was the basis for the Boxer
movement itself. The evidence shows, however, that the
Boxers were not fundamentally a creation of the dynasty.

In 1899 the court made one final major attempt to
prepare for a possible confrontation with the foreign
powers. To strengthen Manchu control over forces in the
capital area, it appointed Jung Lu, grand councilor and ex-
viceroy of Chihli, as commander of all Chinese forces in
the Peking area. These troops formed a new Guards Army

(often called the Grand Army in the West) under the control of the central government. Jung Lu immediately reorganized them into five divisions (actually armies) representing left, right, front, rear, and center. The Front Army, under General Nieh Shih-ch'eng, one of China's finest soldiers, consisted of some thirteen thousand troops to be placed at Lu T'ai, directly north of Taku near the coast. The Left Army, with ten thousand men under General Sung Ch'ing, was to be located at Shanhaikuan, on the northern coast, and would be responsible for protecting the eastern entrance at the Great Wall. Troops for both forces would be recruited from the old Anhui provincial army formed by Li Hung-chang several years earlier, and both would be reorganized along modern lines.

The Rear Army, under the ex-brigand Muslim general Tung Fu-hsiang, was to be located at Tungchow, directly east of the capital. Tung Fu-hsiang's ten thousand men, previously known as the Kansu Army, had the reputation of being ill-disciplined, but good fighters. The Right Army, the Peiyang Army of Yüan Shih-k'ai, was to be based at Hsiao Chan, near Tientsin. At Nan Yüan, just south of Peking, Jung Lu himself would command the Center Army, which consisted primarily of Manchu bannermen. This force would number fewer than ten thousand men. Headquarters for the five armies, which totaled approximately sixty thousand men, was to be located in Peking. Additional troops, most of them under the command of the new Chihli viceroy, Yü Lu, would make the total forces in the metropolitan area approximately ninety thousand.

The formation of the new Guards Army was a major step in the modernization of Chinese military forces. There were already signs, however, that it might not be adequate for the occasion. Foreign military officers who inspected the Chinese troops in the capital area commented on a variety of continuing problems: poor leadership, lack of training, the wide variety of weapons (Ralph Powell, author of *The Rise of Chinese Military Power, 1895-*

1912, says that one unit had fourteen different types of rifles), and those persistent evils, corruption and inadequate pay.

The court also made halting efforts to modernize the military forces elsewhere in China, particularly in those areas considered vital to the defense of the empire— Manchuria, the Yangtse Valley, and the area of the Huai River near Hsüchow. Local autonomy and lack of funding were major obstacles and not much was achieved. In a war against the foreigner, Jung Lu's forces in the metropolitan areas would have to bear the burden of the fighting.

CONDITIONS IN THE CENTER

A decision to resist the foreigner would create an additional and perhaps more serious problem for the court. Peking's belligerent reactions to the activities of the great powers were not echoed with the same intensity in official circles elsewhere in China. To the contrary, many top officials in the central and southern provinces were aghast at the possibility that China would go to war against all the Western powers at the same time. This was certainly the attitude of the two Chinese viceroys in the Yangtse Valley area—Chang Chih-tung, viceroy of Hunan and Hupei, and Liu K'un-yi, viceroy of Kiangsi, Kiangsu, and Anhui; and of Li Hung-chang, viceroy of Kwangtung and Kwangsi provinces in south China. Unlike many of the Manchu noblemen in the north, who had relatively little acquaintance with the West and held a deep-seated suspicion of all things foreign, the Chinese viceroys who ruled the central and southern provinces with considerable autonomy were sophisticated and worldly. They had dealt with the Western nations for several decades and had long believed that, in order for China to survive, it must gain time in which to modernize. To do so China would have to learn to conciliate.[2]

For years Chinese viceroys such as these had held the Manchu empire together. Chang, a native of Chihli, was born in an official family in 1837. He was a bright classical scholar in his youth. At the age of twenty-six he began to show a tendency toward unorthodoxy by concentrating on contemporary problems in the metropolitan examinations for a bureaucratic career. Entering government service in 1867, Chang earned a reputation as a moderate convinced of the need for China to reform in order to compete in the modern world. In 1882 he received his first gubernatorial appointment and quickly showed himself to be a major force for moderate change in China, building arsenals, advocating reform of commerce and industry, and forming the new Self-strengthening Army. Although Chang Chih-tung was more progressive than most of the Manchu aristocrats at court in Peking, he was a cautious man in a crisis, and his loyalty to the dynasty was unquestioned. If he opposed the Boxers, it was because he saw them as a danger to the dynasty, creating an excuse for Western powers to intervene in China to protect the lives of their citizens.[3]

At the time of the crisis, Liu K'un-yi, a Hunanese with thirty-five years of service to the dynasty, was nearing the end of a long and distinguished career. In earlier years he had often been active in diplomatic negotiations and was generally identified with a policy of conciliation. While governor-general of Kiangsi and Kiangsu in the early 1890s, he had severely suppressed antimissionary riots led by secret societies. Earlier considered a conservative on social matters, he had gradually become a cautious supporter of reform.

The final member of the triumvirate, Li Hung-chang, was the most prominent statesman in China during the last quarter of the nineteenth century. From an official family in Anhui Province, he had risen to the vital position of viceroy of Chihli in the 1870s and 1880s. After nearly a half-century of service to the dynasty, he was considered to be one of China's most astute diplomats. While his probity was sometimes questioned, Li was generally thought to be a man with whom Western governments

could negotiate. In 1899, at the age of seventy-six, he was appointed viceroy of the southern provinces of Kwangtung and Kwangsi.

In response to the trouble in the north the court had instructed civil authorities throughout China to put their military forces on a war footing and to resist any attempt at the landing of foreign forces in China. In May 1899 K'ang Yi, antiforeign Manchu nobleman and head of the War Ministry, was sent to central China. His mission was to inspect the defensive conditions in the Yangtse Valley area and to garner financial and political support for the central government from Viceroy Liu K'un-yi. Like Chang Chih-tung and Li Hung-chang, Liu had survived in the bureaucracy by learning how to conciliate influential persons at the court, and he graciously consented to provide funds for the imperial treasury. His opinions on the crisis were another matter, but for the moment he kept them to himself.

Liu K'un-yi might have been willing to make a token gesture to the court in its hour of need, but he and his fellow viceroys were concerned by the drift toward war in the north and they began to consider actions to prevent the spread of the crisis elsewhere in China. As the trouble grew, they attempted to isolate the areas under their control from the antiforeign rioting and to exterminate every manifestation of the Boxer movement throughout central and south China. A few scattered signs of unrest had appeared in these areas, but they could usually be attributed to starvation conditions rather than hostility against foreigners. Once it became evident that the antiforeign contagion had infected the court in Peking, the viceroys began to consider the feasibility of mutual alliances in order to protect themselves from the madness in the north.

THE SEYMOUR EXPEDITION MOVES OUT

Admiral Edward Seymour had the choice of two

Bird's-eye view of the north China plain from the coast to Peking (*Leslie's Weekly*, July 28, 1900, p. 92)

possible routes to cover the sixty-odd miles between Tientsin and Peking. One route followed the bank of the Pei Ho, directly northwest of Tientsin, through the commercial city of Tungchow and thence up to the eastern gates of the capital. The other and more southerly route followed the Tientsin-Peking railroad. North of Tientsin

the rail line followed the east bank of the river up to Yangts'un, where a railroad bridge carried the lines across to the opposite bank. From there the railroad went in a west-northwesterly direction considerably south of the river and eventually connected with the Peking-Hankow line just south of Peking.

Admiral Seymour was aware that the flatlands between Tientsin and the capital were infested with Boxers who had ripped up much of the rail line to Peking. He planned to repair the line en route, thus saving time and avoiding the harsher climate and more difficult terrain of the river route. Still, the area between Tientsin and Peking, primarily flat and sometimes marshy lowlands with scattered villages of mud huts, was almost unbearably hot in the summer of 1900. Seymour's forces would have to trudge through miles of wheat fields in the blistering summer sun.

From the first day it appeared that Seymour had made some questionable assumptions. The two-thousand-man force, traveling in five railroad cars, met little Boxer resistance except for a few skirmishes at the village of Lo Ra.[4] But repair of the railroad line proved time-consuming, and at the end of the first day the expedition had only managed to reach the railroad bridge at Yangts'un, twenty-five miles north of Tientsin. On the morning of June 12, as the allied troop train crossed the railroad bridge to the west bank of the river, Seymour's forces encountered the troops of General Nieh Shih-ch'eng's Front Army. The latter offered no opposition but simply exchanged friendly greetings and taunts.

Problems continued to impede progress, however. Moving westward toward Lang Fang, the expeditionary troops were slowed down by track repairs and constantly harassed by bands of Boxers operating from the wheat fields along the line. By evening they had reached Lang Fang, only halfway from Yangts'un to the capital, which was still forty miles away. Provisions were running short, and Seymour left small detachments of guards at each rail-

way station en route to facilitate the shipment of new supplies up the line.

Seymour hoped to continue on to Peking the next morning, June 13, but reconnaissance units reported that they were unable to penetrate beyond the village of An Ting, only a few miles west of Lang Fang, because of Boxer acitivity. Short of food and water and in need of additional material to repair the rail line, Seymour called a halt and sent back for supplies. Now, however, his troubles began to multiply. Supply trains attempting to return to Tientsin for provisions were forced to turn back because of new destruction on the rail line. Unable to advance toward Peking, and cut off from the rear, Seymour's forces were trapped.

In Peking, reports of the approach of the allied expeditionary force had caused consternation in court circles. The Tsungli Yamen, now controlled by reactionary elements, pleaded with Sir Claude MacDonald to halt Seymour's advance. On the morning of June 13, while Seymour was debating whether to move on toward the capital or to retreat, the court told the legations that the thousand guards already in Peking were more than adequate to guard the diplomatic community and demanded that Seymour's force return to Tientsin. When the ministers refused, the Chinese government realized that open hostilities were inevitable. At a meeting of the Grand Council it was decided that imperial troops would be used to resist the further advance of the allied expeditionary force. Viceroy Yü Lu was ordered to instruct General Nieh Shih-ch'eng to place his troops along the railroad line to guard against any attempt on the part of the Western troops to threaten the capital. At Taku, General Lo Jung-kuang was ordered to be on the alert for any surprise moves by the Western naval forces off the coast. To protect Peking, which now had about five thousand troops under Tung Fu-hsiang and Prince Tuan, the court ordered General Yüan Shih-k'ai to rush his troops to the city.

At Lang Fang, the situation was perilous. Seymour

had seriously underestimated the difficulties he was likely
to encounter on the way to Peking. He was a career naval
officer, with little experience in land warfare, and was
obviously out of his element. Moreover, his capacity to
lead was hampered by the inherent ambiguity of the
situation. As commander of a multinational force, his was
a position of seniority more than of command.

For two days Seymour and his forces remained
stranded at Lang Fang while the admiral attempted to de-
cide what to do. Harassment from Boxer bands armed
with spears, swords, and even clubs did not cause many
casualties—indeed, the losses on the Chinese side were
much greater—but they added to the difficulty of opening
communications with the rear. His reconnaissance forces
had been attacked on June 13 by a Boxer force at An Ting,
and to the rear there had been attacks on the railway
station at the village of Lo Fa, halfway to the railway
bridge at Yangts'un. Later, Seymour would contend that
"an immediate dash to save the legations was the only
course to pursue." At Lang Fang, however, retreat seemed
advisable. On June 15, after one more abortive attempt to
send a supply train back for provisions, Seymour decided
to return to Tientsin on foot.

THE ATTACK ON THE TAKU FORTS

In the warships off the coast at Taku, the news of the
Seymour fiasco caused serious concern. The rumors that
the Chinese government was willing to risk hostilities with
the Western powers now seemed to be proving all too true.
Information from the mainland suggested that the court was
now actively preparing for war. General Nieh Shih-ch'eng,
one source reported, had been instructed to move his
troops toward Taku. Mines were being laid at the mouth of
the Pei Ho to impede the entry of Western ships toward
Tientsin. Rumors abounded that Chinese forces planned
to launch a massive attack on June 19, the anniversary of
the Tientsin massacre of 1870.

On June 16 the admirals decided to take action. At a conference held on the Russian flagship and attended by military commanders of all the powers except the United States, they decided unanimously to send an ultimatum to the Chinese demanding the surrender of the Taku forts which protected the entrance to the Pei Ho. The Chinese fortifications at Taku consisted of several forts lying astride the Pei Ho at the conjunction of the river with the

An artist's view of the Taku forts (*Leslie's Weekly,* July 28, 1900, p. 67)

Gulf of Chihli. They had been destroyed by the allies during the Lorcha Arrow War and rebuilt shortly afterward. If the Chinese did not surrender the forts by 2:00 A.M. the following morning, the powers would open hostilities.

An attack on the Taku forts would be difficult, since the mud flats at the mouth of the river made it impossible for deep-draft warships to approach close enough to the fortifications to bombard them with their heavy guns. The major warships of the powers were forced to remain ten miles away. After dark on the evening of June 16 nine shallow-draft gunboats (French, British, Russian, and German) entered the river and took up positions adjacent to the forts. Just after midnight the Chinese garrison opened fire on the small flotilla in the river. The allied ships responded, and, after several hours of intermittent firing of their light guns, they sent landing parties across

the mud flats to storm the Chinese fortifications. By the early morning hours Chinese resistance had collapsed. With fewer than two hundred casualties (according to one estimate, sixty-four were killed and eighty-nine wounded), the Western powers had won the first major battle of the war. Chinese losses, many of them a result of the allied bombardment which blew up powder magazines within the fortifications, were estimated at three thousand.

The Western assault on Taku settled the gnawing controversy within the Chinese government over whether or not to go to war. Even as late as June 16 the court had considered the possibility of a compromise. At a meeting of the Grand Council on that date, Manchu nobles in attendance were virtually unanimous in advocating firm resistance, but a few councilmen were hesitant, asking how China could expect to resist all the great powers at one time. When K'ang Yi replied that the Boxers were invincible, someone commented that, to the contrary, as a force for the defense of the dynasty they were completely unreliable. It was Tz'u Hsi herself who settled the argument:

If we cannot rely upon the supernatural formulas, can we not rely on the hearts of the people? China is weak; the only thing we can depend on is the heart of the people. If we lose it, how can we maintain our territory?[5]

To her listeners the meaning was clear. By the "hearts of the people" she meant the Boxers.

In the end a compromise was reached. Unaware that Seymour's forces had already retreated, the council sent two men to persuade the admiral to return to Tientsin. In the likely event that this bid for peace was unsuccessful (and it was: the two emissaries were unable to get through and were forced to return to the capital), preparations would be made for war. Viceroy Yü Lu and the generals in the capital area were instructed to resist any attempt by Western forces to approach Peking. Similar instructions were sent to General Tseng Ch'i in Manchuria, where Russian troops were massing. Moreover, the council made the fateful decision to incorporate Boxer units into the regular army. The Boxers were now formally to be considered defenders of the state.

Events were now in motion that made war inevitable. On June 17 the empress dowager summoned the members of the Grand Council and announced that she had just received a four-point ultimatum from the great powers. As conditions for a peace settlement, the foreigners were demanding that a special residence be set aside for the emperor; all revenues of the Chinese empire be collected by the foreign legations; and all military affairs be placed under foreign control. The ultimatum made a fourth demand, most significant of all, which Tz'u Hsi did not announce at the time but which would come out later: Tz'u Hsi was to abdicate her position and the emperor was to be restored to active rule.

The ultimatum was obviously designed to humiliate the court. Indeed, its fourth demand attacked the empress dowager where she was most vulnerable. Tz'u Hsi played the situation to the hilt. She was outraged at the effrontery of the barbarians in their attempt to interfere in the internal affairs of the Celestial Empire. If the court accepted such demands, China could not survive, she declared. Should we not fight to our last breath? she ranted. When one of her advisers brought out a declaration of war that had been drafted earlier, she approved it on the spot.

Most members of the council were too cowed by Tz'u Hsi's imperious behavior to question her decisions. Jung Lu was not, however. Absolutely loyal to the empress dowager and long a favorite at court, he was allowed, within limits, to raise objections. Jung Lu had not reached and maintained his position of influence without learning the limits of his power, however, and he exercised his privilege with caution. In this case, he was troubled because Tz'u Hsi's plans appeared to include a direct attack on the foreign ministries. War was one thing, but an attack on the legation quarter was another, and Jung Lu appealed to the empress dowager not to permit it. To attempt to kill a diplomatic representative, he pointed out, was to insult a country. If the foreign ministers in Peking were massacred, all of the great powers would unite in a war of revenge against China.

Jung Lu received some support from others at court. Hsü Ching-ch'eng, ex-minister to the tsarist court at St. Petersburg and now head of the Imperial University in Peking, and Yüan Ch'ang, a minister in the Tsungli Yamen, pleaded for caution. The latter argued that the ultimatum had to be a forgery, since the foreign diplomats were too experienced to believe they could interfere so blatantly in the affairs of the empire. Moreover, he said, it would be folly to rely on the so-called "magical powers" of the Boxers. He had himself visited the legation quarter and seen the bodies of Boxer troops who had been repelled by foreign bullets. So much for the vaunted invulnerability of these "defenders of the dynasty."

The pleas of the moderates aroused Tz'u Hsi's anger. She declared that she had taken all that she could stand from the barbarian devils and commanded Jung Lu and his allies to hold their tongues. She did agree, however, to hold off on a declaration of war and to send an ultimatum demanding that the foreign envoys and their families leave China. In the meantime she ordered Yüan Shih-k'ai to send units of his Peiyang Army to the capital in preparation for possible hostilities. Representatives from the Tsungli Yamen were sent to inform the legations that, if the Western powers wanted war, the diplomatic corps would have to leave China. Sir Claude MacDonald answered for the allies. Admiral Seymour was not coming to Peking with hostile intentions, he said, but solely to protect the lives of the foreign residents in the capital. MacDonald would not agree to halt the relieving force.

The ministers were puzzled by the Chinese ultimatum, for the so-called "four-point ultimatum" received by Tz'u Hsi had not been sent by the allies but was indeed a forgery, concocted by Prince Tuan and his allies to incite the empress dowager to declare war on the barbarians. When Jung Lu learned, a few days after its receipt, that the document was spurious, he informed Tz'u Hsi. She launched a tirade against the perpetrators, but by then it was too late to avoid the consequences.

Still, although war seemed imminent, neither side had irrevocably opened hostilities. The Western assault on Taku settled the issue. On June 19, when the court received a memorial from Yü Lu reporting the Western ultimatum to surrender the Taku forts, Tz'u Hsi concluded that the powers were determined to resort to force. The legations were informed that diplomatic relations were broken, and the foreigners were told to leave the city within twenty-four hours.

On the same day China declared war on the foreign powers.[6] Imperial troops were given a free hand to open attacks on all foreign forces in north China. Prince Chuang and K'ang Yi were appointed to command the Boxer forces—thirty thousand strong in the Peking area alone. An additional forty-four hundred units, each consisting of up to several hundred men, were assigned to Prince Tuan to guard the capital.

SEYMOUR RETURNS TO TIENTSIN

Admiral Seymour's plan for the return to Tientsin was to retreat to Yangts'un by rail, repairing the line on the way, and then to reorganize his forces for an advance upriver. From Yangts'un he hoped to find junks to transport heavy weapons and the wounded back to Tientsin via the Pei Ho. The remainder of the military column would accompany the junks along the west bank.

By June 18 the retreating columns had managed to return to the rail-river junction at Yangts'un. On the way from Lang Fang they had been constantly exposed to attacks by the Boxers. Moreover, the German units deployed to protect the rear of the column were harassed by five thousand imperial troops under the command of General Tung Fu-hsiang. This was the first time that regular troops had engaged in open combat with Seymour's forces.

At Yangts'un Seymour abandoned the train and seized several native boats for transporting the wounded, provisions, heavy field guns, and ammunition. In mid-afternoon of June 19 the allied units began moving downriver. Unfortunately, the drought throughout north China had caused the river level to drop, and the seized junks had trouble navigating. This problem was compounded by the Westerners' lack of familiarity with the unwieldy Chinese river craft. At the beginning of the march all the heavy equipment had to be left behind. Soon the junks were abandoned entirely and the wounded were forced to join the rest of the troops along the river bank. As the forces progressed, they cleared the Boxers by rifle and bayonet from several villages along the way. At the end of the first day they had traveled only eight miles toward Tientsin and relative safety.

Progress over the next few days continued to be agonizingly slow, and by the afternoon of June 21 the advance units reached the Hsi-ku arsenal on the west bank of the river about three miles north of Tientsin. The allied units were short of ammunition as well as food and water; the arsenal was a welcome sight. In late afternoon two groups of allied forces, one British and the other German, crossed the river and seized the arsenal with little opposition. Inside they found several guns and over fifteen tons of rice. Seymour decided to spend the night at Hsi-ku. He sent out several messengers to inform the allied forces in Tientsin that his troops were just north of the city, but none was able to get through.

Secure in the arsenal, Seymour decided to remain at Hsi-ku, care for the wounded, and await assistance. On June 23 Chinese forces tried to retake the arsenal, but the defenders, well armed and well stocked once again, were able to repel them. Captured Chinese soldiers reported that General Nieh Shih-ch'eng's army was discouraged. It had attacked Seymour's small units with twenty-five battalions for several days without success. A total of 62 of Seymour's forces had been killed and about 230 wounded.

On June 25 help for Seymour's besieged forces finally arrived. Nearly two thousand Russian troops under Colonel

Shirinsky, newly arrived from Port Arthur, moved upriver from Tientsin and relieved Seymour's garrison. After destroying the arsenal, all units returned to the city of Tientsin.

AMERICA ENTERS THE CONFLICT

The attack on the Chinese fortifications at Taku had been a joint action of all the powers present off the north China coast except the United States. Throughout the planning and military phase the Americans had held themselves aloof. On June 14, when queried by the British as to American plans in the event of hostilities at Taku, Admiral Louis Kempff, highest ranking officer in the American squadron, had replied that he was "not authorized to initiate any act of war with a country with which my country is at peace." The next day, when allied forces occupied the railway station near the forts in preparation for the eventual move to Tientsin, American troops had not participated in the operation, nor had they taken part in the actual attack on Taku. Admiral Kempff had taken literally Hay's June 10 telegram to Conger calling for a cautious policy in China. Kempff did send upriver the American warship *Monocacy,* a gunboat built during the Civil War, to provide a shelter for the foreign community at Taku during the bombardment. Ironically, it was the first ship to be struck by Chinese shells during the assault on the forts.

Admiral Kempff's attitude reflected the McKinley administration's caution regarding the crisis. The first reactions to Kempff's reticence in the American press were somewhat critical; some observers remembered that another American naval commander in China, faced with a similar situation, had said, "Blood is thicker than water," and joined in an allied naval operation against the forts. [7] Even President McKinley questioned Kempff's decision, but he soon revised his opinion. In a message to Congress he stated that a hostile demonstration by the powers

Cartoon of Uncle Sam and President McKinley attacking the murderous Boxers, entitled "Is this Imperialism?" (*Harper's Weekly*, August 28, 1900, cover)

would simply serve to intensify antiforeign feeling in China and encourage the Boxers to take action against Seymour's relief force. And, of course, American participation would have unleashed widespread criticism of the administration's misuse of executive authority to launch yet another imperialist adventure.

Still, McKinley's administration had been sufficiently concerned about events in north China to make some preparations for possible hostilities. In early June a battalion of the 1st Marines was dispatched from Cavite in the

Philippines, arriving off Taku on June 18. On June 16 the
9th Infantry Regiment under Colonel Emerson Liscum was
ordered from Manila; it was due to arrive in China on July 6,
to be followed shortly by the 6th U.S. Cavalry, scheduled
to embark from San Francisco on July 1. These moves
were officially interpreted as missions to protect American
lives and property, not as acts of war. Hay still sought to
draw a clear distinction between joint military action and
American diplomatic action.

The ambivalence within the McKinley administration
accurately reflected the mood throughout the country.
On the one hand a rising wave of anti-imperialism was
sweeping the nation. The takeover of the Philippines at the
end of the Spanish-American War and American actions
against the Filipino forces of Emilio Aguinaldo north of
Manila had inspired a distaste for colonial activity among
a significant proportion of the nation's citizens. Any belli-
cose action by American forces in China would certainly
be interpreted in these circles as the beginning of a new
American adventure in Asia. To a considerable extent,
these anti-imperialist views were taken up by the Democratic
party, in opposition since the ascent of McKinley to the
presidency in 1896. This was undoubtedly a factor in dam-
pening the enthusiasm of some groups in the Republican
party for further action in China during the first weeks of
summer.

Indeed, vociferous forces within the country were
prodding the administration to take stern action to protect
American interests in China. The strongest advocates of an
active posture, perhaps, were religious groups involved in
the missionary effort which was now imperiled by Boxer
activities in north China. If McKinley did not act to protect American missionaries, a French diplomatic observer
warned, he would be the object of "Biblical maledictions"
from every pulpit in America. More broadly, of course, an
active American foreign policy in Asia had support from
many groups throughout the country, not least in the
"yellow press" which had been partly responsible for fo-

menting the just-completed war against Spain. As one
popular American weekly of the period commented, "That
America, once having decided to move, is to back up her
plan, whatever it is, with enough troops and ships is gratifying to everyone in the East. Let those who are inclined
to cavil at the new role of the country in the world's
affairs remember that the moment is rapidly approaching,
if it has not arrived, when the future of the world's civilization will be at stake. Will it be a world in which the
English-speaking race, with its high standard of life and
liberty, will prevail; or a world in which the despot and the
slave—shall we leave out the 'e' and call it Slav?—will
dictate the future of the sphere?"[8] It was under the influence of such criticism in the press that McKinley had reluctantly dispatched the 9th Infantry Regiment from the
Philippines to north China. In a private discussion with
French Ambassador Cambon, Secretary Hay said that the
regiment would be the last American unit to be sent to
the area. Time would show that this was an unduly optimistic assessment of the situation.

THE VICEROYS STRUGGLE FOR PEACE

In central and south China, the viceroys viewed the
escalation of the crisis with increasing nervousness. When
the situation deteriorated, moderates in Peking under Jung
Lu attempted to persuade Liu K'un-yi to intercede along
with Li Hung-chang, probably the man with the most influence at court, to encourage the empress dowager to suppress the Boxers. Li, however, was a cautious man during
a crisis. He refused Liu K'un-yi's invitation to take action,
saying that, since the empress dowager was for the moment
determined on her course of action, any persuasion on his
part would be futile. Rebuffed by Li Hung-chang, Liu
K'un-yi turned to Chang Chih-tung, and on June 14 the
two sent a joint memorial to Peking urging the suppres-
sion of the antiforeign movement and suggesting that Li
Hung-chang be appointed to negotiate a settlement with

the great powers. Otherwise, they warned, China would be subjected to a disastrous foreign invasion. Unfortunately, the memorial did not arrive until after the fall of the Taku forts. By then it was too late to avert war.

Once war had been declared on the powers, of course, the viceroys found themselves in a delicate situation. Any move on their part to conciliate the foreigners could be interpreted by the court as treason. Still, convinced that war was futile, they were inclined to do their best to ignore the declaration of war and to avoid hostilities in areas under their control. They did not publicize the government's edict and increasingly drew together for mutual support.

The desire for compromise on the part of the viceroys did not go unnoticed in Western capitals, and soon after the brief Taku campaign the Western naval commanders in north China issued a statement designed to assuage their concern:

The admirals and senior naval officers of the allied powers in China desire to make known to all viceroys and authorities of the coasts and rivers, cities and provinces of China that they intend to use armed force only against Boxers and people who oppose them on their march to Peking for the rescue of their fellow-countrymen.[9]

For their part, in other words, the allies did not consider themselves to be at war with China.

The viceroys rushed to take advantage of this conciliatory statement, and jointly memorialized the throne to suppress the Boxer movement in north China. Liu told Jung Lu that he would be willing to march north to fight for his country, but that to slaughter a few helpless foreigners would be an act "totally lacking in humanity." The thrust of their memorial thus paralleled that of the admirals' statement, and for emphasis the viceroys sent copies to world capitals.

The viceroys' attempts to isolate the rest of China from the unrest in Chihli Province met with the general approval of the foreign community in central and south

China. The trouble in the north had had a noticeable effect in the Yangtse Valley area—trade had slowed down, factories stood idle, and steamship service to other areas of the nation had been discontinued. To reassure the local populace, the foreign consuls issued a statement declaring their willingness to cooperate with the local authorities in maintaining law and order. Foreign warships in the Shanghai harbor (there were eight at the time) took up positions for possible action as "a measure of precaution," but avoided hostile actions. The British consul-general in Shanghai offered troops to help suppress antiforeign activities, but the local authorities rejected assistance, stating that such foreign aid would only "inflame the situation."

In response to these gestures from the foreign powers, the viceroys decided to offer to keep the peace by their own actions throughout the Yangtse Valley if the powers would agree to maintain order in the foreign concessions area in Shanghai. On June 26 the viceroys presented the foreign consuls with a nine-point draft proposal calling for mutual efforts to maintain peace in the area. The consuls objected to only one point in the proposal—that the viceroys would not be held responsible for disturbances caused by the entrance of foreign warships in the Yangtse River unless the ships' entry had been sanctioned by them. On June 27 the consuls responded by saying that they had no intention of landing forces in the Yangtse Valley so long as the rights of foreigners throughout the area were maintained, but that they demanded the right to take whatever action was necessary to rescue foreigners subjected to threats from antiforeign elements.

So long as the area remained quiet, the problem was hypothetical. Still, unless something could be done to halt war in the north, local measures to limit the spread of hostilities would probably prove futile. Obviously, the viceroys, while doing their best to exert a calming influence in Peking, would have to open private communications with foreign capitals to assure them that a negotiated settlement was indeed a possibility. Li Hung-chang gave active consideration during the last week of June to making a trip north to argue for compromise. Though he did not follow through on this plan, he did, on his own initiative and without informing Peking, send telegrams to foreign powers assuring them that the action at Taku had not been ordered by Peking, and asking them if at all possible to keep diplomatic communications open with the Chinese government.

Chang Chih-tung pursued the will-of-the-wisp of peace through his own contacts in Japan. He suggested to Tokyo that, if the great powers agreed not to advance beyond Tientsin or to threaten the capital, the empress dowager would be assured of their peaceful intentions and would then be able to suppress the Boxers and their supporters at court.

In Peking the moderates were not so optimistic. Late in June Jung Lu wrote to Chang Chih-tung confiding that he and his allies, Prince Ch'ing and Wang Wen-shao, had no influence over the militants who were now strongly in control at court. One moderate in the government was so discouraged about the trends in Peking that he asked Yüan Shih-k'ai, governor of Shantung Province, to march on Peking and stage a coup to get rid of the militants. Yüan had been firmly suppressing antiforeign activities in Shantung and was considered an ally of the moderate faction. But when he was asked to dispatch some of his best troops to Peking, he found excuses for delay. Yüan was solicitous of his own neck and sensed that the time for decisive action was not yet ripe. The problem at Peking was internal, he replied, and required internal treatment. With obvious reluctance, he eventually did send a newly organized unit, but it arrived too late to affect the fighting there.

Chapter Six

The Siege at Peking

While generals and diplomats in world capitals pondered over what action to take in China, the residents of the legation quarter watched with mounting anxiety as their last ties to the outside world were broken. By the second week in June Peking seemed on the verge of chaos. Boxers were entering the capital by the thousands. They wandered at will through the city looting and burning, inflamed to a fever pitch of anti-Western feeling. According to observers, many were youths from the neighboring villages; others appeared to be regulars of Tung Fu-hsiang's Kansu Army. The latter had apparently come to the city at the express will of the empress dowager.

The government seemed powerless—or reluctant—to take action to maintain law and order. Since the rampaging Boxer squads made no distinction between high and low status, native or foreigner, those inhabitants of the city who could afford to do so began to leave, taking their precious belongings with them. Terror and violence ruled the streets of Peking.

Indeed, the impression that the court had no intention of curbing the violence was not far from the truth.
As the crisis worsened, the empress dowager appeared
content to let events unfold unchecked and to give the
militants free rein. In fact, two of the leading antiforeign
officials at court, K'ang Yi and Duke Lan, had actually attended the conflagration at the Christian church on the
night of June 13, and Tz'u Hsi had watched from the imperial palace as the flames brightened the night sky.

As the noose tightened around them, the foreigners
tried to strike back. Scouting parties sent out by the legations frequently encountered and attacked roving bands of
Boxers on the streets of Peking. On one occasion a patrol
composed of American, British, and Japanese soldiers discovered a group of several dozen Boxers looting a temple
in the eastern section of the city (one source says the foreigners broke in while the Boxers were preparing Chinese
Christians for human sacrifice on an altar). According to
the somewhat laconic account by Lancelot Giles, a student
interpreter at the British legation, every one of the Boxers
was killed "almost without resistance."[1]

Attacks on that scale were hardly sufficient, however,
to protect the foreigners from the seemingly thousands of
Chinese stirred to an anti-Western frenzy by the Boxer
activities and the attitude of the court. Indeed, sober heads
in the diplomatic community were painfully aware of their
vulnerability to attack. They were isolated in an inland
capital over a hundred miles from the sea; they were
viewed with increasing hostility by the local populace and
by the Chinese government, whose own intentions were
shrouded in mystery; and their entire armed force consisted of fewer than five hundred officers and enlisted men
of mixed nationalities.

Not the least of the foreigners' problems was the relative indefensibility of the legation quarter itself. Backed on
the south by the Peking city wall—a brick rampart fifty
feet high and approximately forty feet thick which surrounded the entire Tartar city—the diplomatic quarter

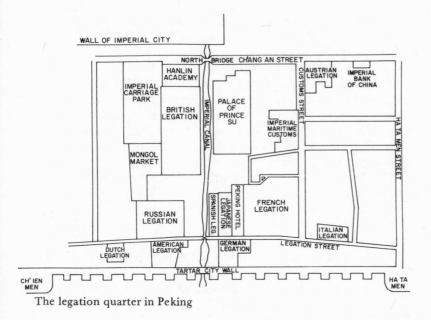

The legation quarter in Peking

comprised an area a bit more than two thousand feet square. The city wall to the south offered some protection, but the remaining three sides were open to street traffic and were dangerously vulnerable to attack from the outside. Along the eastern and western boundaries, though, there were several features which might be utilized to form a defensive perimeter. On the east the French and German legations and the building housing the Imperial Maritime Customs were all stout edifices that could form the cornerstones of a defensive line running along Omann Street, one of the major north-south thoroughfares in the city. The two legations located east of this line—Austrian and Italian—presumably would have to be evacuated. Along the western boundary the backs of the Russian and British legations and, at the juncture of the wall, the Russo-Chinese Bank formed a natural defense line against attack. To the west of this line was the imperial carriage park and a small Mongol market; these would have to be cleared to provide adequate visibility for the defenders against any attacking force. Beyond the market and the carriage park were some of the major ministries of the Chinese empire, along with the legation of the Netherlands, which was too isolated to be given adequate protection. To make the eastern and western perimeters reasonably secure from attack, the foreigners would have to block off the street accesses to the legation quarter. The main problem was Legation Street, which ran directly through the quarter about six hundred feet north of the wall.

Another difficult task for the foreigners would be the defense of the northern perimeter. The northern boundary was Ch'ang An Street, a major thoroughfare which ran along the south wall of the imperial city. It offered easy access to the heart of the legation quarter, particularly in the center where the imperial canal ran directly south from the imperial city to exit at a water gate along the Tartar wall. If attackers penetrated into the legation area along the canal, they could split the quarter in half. In that event defense of the legations would be a virtual impossibility.

Even along the south wall the defenders faced no easy task, for along the top of the wall ran a parapet about forty feet wide. To protect the legations the foreigners would have to control the wall virtually from the Ch'ien Men in the center to the Ha Ta Men, about halfway from the Ch'ien Men to the southeastern corner of the Tartar city. If the attackers gained control of the wall, they would be able to rain rifle and cannon fire at will into the heart of the diplomatic quarter.

Even if the foreigners had been able to secure a defensive position, their weaponry would have proved inadequate to the task. The only fieldpiece available was an Italian one-pounder which, although accurate enough, could do little damage, since its shells were so small. In addition, there were a few rapid-fire machine guns—the Americans had a Colt, the Austrians a Maxim, and the British an old five-barrel Nordenfeldt which often failed to

The Catholic Peitang Cathedral in Peking, refuge of Bishop Favier and the Chinese Christians during the siege (*Leslie's Weekly,* August 18, 1900, p. 128)

work. Ammunition was in relatively short supply, and certainly not sufficient for a long siege.

The population of the foreign community numbered slightly more than 470, including 149 women and 79 children. The quarter was guarded by a military contingent of approximately 450 men, 21 of them officers of various nationalities. The largest forces—slightly over 80 each—were the British and the Russians. There were 56 Americans and about an equal number of Germans, 75 French, 37 Austrians, 39 Italians, and 25 Japanese. Of this number, 43 had been sent to the Peitang Cathedral to guard the Roman Catholic converts there. This total, absurdly inadequate to protect the quarter from the several thousand regular troops and Boxers at large within the city, would eventually be supplemented by 75 civilian volunteers recruited from among the 245 male residents. Called the "Carving Knife Brigade" in reference to the variety of weapons at their disposal, this ragtag group performed valuable service in the defense of the legations throughout the siege.

THE BEGINNING OF THE SIEGE

At four o'clock on the afternoon of June 19 Tz'u Hsi made her official response to the allied attack on the Taku forts. At that hour all the foreign legations received identical messages from the Tsungli Yamen: because of the attack on Taku, a state of war existed between China and the powers. The diplomatic representatives and all of their dependents were instructed to leave Peking within twenty-four hours and retire to Tientsin, from whence they could be evacuated from China. Recognizing the danger of attack, the Tsungli Yamen (prompted by Jung Lu, who had pleaded with the empress dowager to recognize that the sanctity of diplomatic representatives was a cardinal point of agreement among the nations of the world) offered to provide an armed guard to escort the foreigners to safety.

The diplomatic community was divided on how to react to the Chinese ultimatum. Many strongly suspected the court's motives, and some were absolutely opposed to trusting its guarantee of protection. After heated discussion, the ministers decided to play for time. They refused to move from Peking until more guards were provided for their protection, and they demanded an interview with the Tsungli Yamen for the following day. Early the next morning, June 20, the ministers of the various legations gathered at the French Legation. By 9:30 A.M. they had received no reply from the Chinese government on their request for an interview, and the German minister, Baron Klemens von Ketteler, announced that he would go alone to the office of the Tsungli Yamen, several blocks to the northeast of the legation quarter, to obtain an answer. Von Ketteler's behavior was no surprise to his colleagues. Since his arrival in Peking he had earned a reputation for swagger and arrogance. A few days earlier a Boxer had driven a cart into the legation quarter and begun to insult the foreign bystanders while making threatening gestures with his knife. While most had watched nervously, von Ketteler had marched out into the street and begun flailing at the Chinese with his cane until the latter fled.

Von Ketteler's fellow ministers made a half-hearted effort to dissuade him from going, but failed, and von Ketteler and his interpreter, Heinrich Cordes, left in two covered sedan chairs to make their way to the Chinese foreign office. As they passed north on Ha Ta Men Street with von Ketteler in the lead, a Manchu soldier standing alongside the road suddenly pointed his rifle into the minister's chair and fired. Von Ketteler was killed instantly. Cordes, to the rear, froze in horror, then jumped from his own chair and ran. He was wounded by rifle fire in both legs but managed to stumble through the tangled web of streets to the American Methodist Mission, about a mile to the east of the legation quarter. When word of the murder reached the diplomats, they were outraged. A search party was immediately sent out to locate von Ketteler's corpse and bring it back to the German legation, but Chinese soldiers refused to let the foreign troops look for the body, which in any case had disappeared.

Until von Ketteler's murder the envoys had been badly divided on whether to evacuate the foreign community to Tientsin. American Minister Edwin Conger, in particular, was seriously considering accepting the Chinese offer and ordered American families to prepare for departure. He began making these arrangements despite pleas from his subordinates that a foreign exodus from Peking would place the thousands of Chinese Christians in the capital area (including several hundred at the American Methodist Mission) at the mercy of the enraged Boxer hordes rampaging through the streets.

The murder of von Ketteler settled the issue. There would be no movement without adequate protection provided by the allied armed forces. It was now strongly suspected that the German minister's murder had not been an accident, but had been deliberately planned by the court. (Evidence eventually suggested that there was at least some justification for this belief. Several months later German troops apprehended a Manchu soldier who confessed to the slaying; the soldier claimed that his superior officers offered him a reward for shooting the minister. By then the point was somewhat academic. In any event, he was executed on the spot where von Ketteler's murder had taken place.) In the afternoon of June 20 the Tsungli Yamen sent a note to the legations, inviting the ministers to reconsider the ultimatum and to consider means of leaving the capital. The note made no reference to the killing of the German diplomat.

In all probability the murder of von Ketteler played a significant role in the crisis. Whether or not it had been deliberately planned by court reactionaries, von Ketteler's murder was not simply one more step in a rapidly deteriorating situation. China had now committed an irrevocable action: it had inflicted harm on a diplomatic representative of one of the great powers. There appeared now no way out of the stand-off short of war. At 4:00 P.M. on June 21, when the twenty-four-hour ultimatum expired, Chinese troops opened fire on the legations. The siege at Peking had begun.

PREPARATIONS FOR DEFENSE

Within the legations there was no further excuse for delay. During the preceding days flimsy barricades had been erected on the major thoroughfares through the legation quarter and at the bridge crossing the Imperial Canal on Ch'ang An Street along the northern rim of the area. The foreigners now set to work to strengthen their defenses. Sandbags and paving blocks were hastily brought up to strengthen the barriers between the quarter and the outside world. Bomb shelters were built to protect troops along the defensive perimeter, and loopholes were cut in walls to permit the besieged forces to fire on the surrounding Chinese troops.

Other serious problems besides defense strategies

demanded immediate attention. The extent of the foreigners' responsibility for the fate of the Chinese converts at the American Methodist Mission had been argued fiercely within the diplomatic community. Now that the foreigners were going to stay, the converts would not be abandoned, willy-nilly, to the vicissitudes of fate. Still, should they be protected by the legations? American Minister Conger, whose behavior in this respect shamed many of his countrymen in Peking, ordered that the American missionaries at the mission be escorted to the legation quarter for protection, but that the Chinese Christians there—over eight hundred—be instructed to fend for themselves.

Fortunately for the latter, more humane counsel prevailed, and it was finally agreed that the converts would be brought to the quarter and housed in the palace of Prince Su—the Su Wang Fu—a spacious structure directly across the Imperial Canal from the British legation. A party of twenty American marines was dispatched to the mission during a lull in the firing that first afternoon. They escorted the entire party—seventy foreign missionaries and some eight hundred Chinese—to the legation quarter without incident. The Chinese joined more than two thousand converts already huddled together in the palace—all dependent for their survival on the ability of their foreign protectors to stave off the impending attacks. On the following day the American mission and two of the abandoned legations beyond the foreign defense perimeter were burned to the ground.

Once the initial steps had been taken to block off points of easy access to the quarter, the major problem for the foreign community was lack of organization. In light of the diversity of the population within the legation quarter, and of the bitter internecine quarrels that divided the various powers, organizing for defense was no easy matter. First to be decided was the question of leadership. Defense of the legations obviously required the specialized experience of a trained military expert; yet, according to protocol, it was the minister who had the primary responsibility for the protection of all national interests, including the lives and property of all citizens residing in the area. Fortunately, a few of the diplomats present had prior military experience: British Minister Sir Claude MacDonald had been a career officer in the Scot's Greys before entering the diplomatic service, and American Minister Edwin Conger was an ex-infantry officer who had seen combat experience during the Civil War. Also, Conger's first secretary, Herbert Squiers, had served fifteen years in the U.S. cavalry.

Given the circumstances, however, it is hardly surprising that there was a certain period of experimentation before a reasonably stable chain of command was established within the besieged area. At the outset, command was seized by the highest ranking military officer among the foreign community—the Austrian naval officer von Thomann, commander of the Austrian cruiser *Zenta*. Von Thomann happened to be in Peking on vacation when the crisis erupted. As events would prove, he was not a fortuitous choice for leadership, but the other military officers within the quarter were all younger men of low rank and not enough experience to take command.

No amount of combat experience, however, would have eased the precarious situation in which the besieged foreigners found themselves. The military problems of providing for the defense of the legation quarter seemed nearly insurmountable. In addition, there were problems of food and water, of shelter and sanitation, and of dealing with nearly three thousand Chinese crammed into the palace of Prince Su. Here the organizational abilities of Sir Claude MacDonald were quickly demonstrated. As *doyen* of the diplomatic corps in Peking and representative of the premier imperialist power in Asia, MacDonald easily claimed the civilian leadership of the foreign colony. He immediately began to form a committee structure to put some order into the defense of the legations. Committees were also formed to take responsibility for all the

Meeting these needs, of course, required a lot of heavy work—sandbags had to be filled, earthworks constructed, and supplies and ammunition transported. Here the diversity of the community became apparent, and no little grumbling ensued. The Chinese converts were required to provide two hours of work a day and performed most of the manual labor. After the Chinese—many of whom were extremely weak because of poor nutrition—the hardest workers in the foreign community were the missionaries. Trained in self-sufficiency and inured to hardship, the missionaries, led by Tewkesbury and the redoubtable Gamewell, led the way in organizing the defense of the community and, with their energy and their generally unflagging good spirits, set an example for the rest of the colony. Least helpful, according to firsthand accounts, were the diplomats themselves. Class prejudice was still strong, particularly among the Europeans, and many of the legation personnel considered themselves to be above menial labor.

Not only did many of the diplomats refuse to take an active part in the defense, they often allocated to themselves the best food. One of the most shameful facts of the entire siege was the community's mistreatment of the Chinese Christians. Crammed together in the Su Wang Fu, the converts were given little food and to a considerable degree were left to fend for themselves. A few observers in the diplomatic community later wrote sympathetically of the terrible living conditions the converts had to endure throughout the siege. This aspect of the experience unfortunately refuted the common assumption that hardship ennobles those who live through it.

PROTECTING THE LEGATIONS

Given the petty jealousies within the foreign community, it was probably inevitable that the legations would find it difficult to agree on a centralized command structure. For lack of a better solution, they decided to divide the responsibilities, each assigning its own national detachment, where feasible, to protect the area around its legation. The Russians and Americans, because their legations were close to the Tartar city wall, were given primary responsibility for protecting the southern perimeter of the quarter. Aided by Chinese converts, who laboriously carried sandbags up the forty-foot ramps to the top of the wall, the Russians and the Americans erected barricades and assigned units to protect the wall from Chinese attacks.

The French, Germans, and Austrians were assigned primary responsibility for protecting the east flank; the British were to guard their own legation, which overlooked the northwestern boundary of the quarter; and the Japanese, whose own legation was located within the interior of the defense perimeter, were to defend the Su Wang Fu, a key position on the northeast corner.

The compound of the British legation became the inner fortress of the foreign community for the duration of the siege. Most of the foreign community would gather here, since the area was reasonably well protected from external assault and, by virtue of its central location, relatively free of the danger of heavy bombardment. The compound was transformed into the headquarters of the resistance and became the residence for most of the foreign community. A few chose to remain in their own legations or in the Hotel du Pékin, adjacent to the French legation near the eastern edge of the quarter. Within the main building of the British legation, each nation was assigned a room or a suite of rooms, while one wing was blocked off as a hospital, staffed by medical missionaries and women volunteers. Since the main building was intended to be the last redoubt of the defenders should the remainder of the quarter be seized, all the windows and doors were buttressed by sandbags. The residents knew that, if the onslaught reached that point, total defeat would be only a matter of time.

Disagreements among the defenders in the legation

compound began to occur almost at once. In fact, it was
after one particularly acrimonious meeting that Austrian
commander von Thomann had taken command. But,
under the strained circumstances, von Thomann did not
last long. His naval experience proved inadequate for the
military requirements of the moment, and it shortly became evident that he lacked the leadership qualities needed
to handle the crisis. During a brief lull in the fighting on
the morning of June 22 von Thomann was informed that
the American troops on the Tartar wall had abandoned
their positions. Such a move could have been disastrous to
the defense of the quarter. In panic, the Austrian commander ordered a general retreat, calling all remaining
forces to evacuate their positions along the perimeter and
fall back to the British legation. Seeing the activity, the
Russians and the Americans on the wall (who were actually still at their posts behind the barricades) descended
in a disorderly scramble into the compound. Of all the
military forces defending the legation quarter, only the
British along the northern boundary remained at their
posts.

Had the Chinese been prepared to take advantage of
the unexpected confusion in the ranks of the foreigners,
they could have stormed the quarter, bringing the siege to
an abrupt close. Fortunately for the defenders, however,
the Chinese command itself appeared confused by the
movement on the other side of the barricades and took no
action. By the time they realized what had happened, it
was too late. The error was soon corrected, and the troops
returned to their posts.

This near catastrophe vividly demonstrated the need
for cool leadership. Von Thomann was quickly dismissed
and replaced by Sir Claude MacDonald who, as British
minister and a man of considerable combat experience,
seemed to be the natural man for the job. From this point
until the end of the siege, the burdens of the command
rested on MacDonald's shoulders. His position was not an
enviable one. After three days of intermittent hostilities,

the pattern of the siege was beginning to take shape. The foreigners had already been compelled to abandon four of their legations and a part of their defense perimeter on the eastern boundary of the quarter. Sporadic attacks had succeeded in forcing the defenders back from the Austrian and Italian legations as well as the Imperial Maritime Customs. The Chinese were now in a position to concentrate their attacks on the two remaining keystones of the foreigners' eastern line of defense—the French legation and the Su Wang Fu. Although their attacks were often poorly coordinated, in sheer numbers and firepower the Chinese appeared to have an overwhelming advantage. It must have seemed to them that the legations would not be able to hold out for long.

On June 23, the day after the von Thomann fiasco, the Chinese chose to concentrate their attacks on the northern perimeter. Directly to the north of the British compound, between the Imperial Canal and the carriage park, was the famous Hanlin Academy. The academy had one of the best libraries of Chinese historical works, including the sole existing copy of the famous *Yung Lo Ta Tien,* an encyclopedia of some twenty-three thousand volumes dating from the Ming dynasty. In the attacks of the twenty-third, the academy was set afire and burned.

The motives appeared to be primarily military—to level the academy buildings in order to obtain easier access to the north wall surrounding the grounds of the British legation. Once aware of the spreading blaze, the foreigners made strenuous efforts to put out the fire—although one cynical observer contended that many of the fire fighters were more interested in obtaining "souvenirs" than in saving the library—and finally managed to extinguish the flames. Later in the day, however, Tung Fu-hsiang's Kansu soldiers returned to complete the destruction. By the next day the venerable academy and its precious contents were only a heap of smoldering ashes.

Confusion exists as to the court's reaction to the destruction of the priceless library and its artifacts. Some

sources maintain that the empress dowager approved of
the attack, while another contends that when Tz'u Hsi
heard of the conflagration she "showed great anger" at
General Tung Fu-hsiang, whom she considered responsible
for the decision.[2]

The attack on the Hanlin Academy was followed by
several unsuccessful attempts by the Chinese to set fires
along the western perimeter. Despite the fact that the
defenders had to rely on primitive fire fighting equipment, including a bucket brigade from the nearest of the
eight wells in the compound, all the fires were put out
without extensive damage.

In the meantime, pressure was building at the Su
Wang Fu. The Fu was defended by a small contingent of
twenty-three Japanese sailors and eighteen volunteers
under the leadership of the intrepid and resourceful Major
Shiba, Japanese military attaché in Peking. It was an integral part of the legations' defense lines, and a forced
retreat from the building would have been disastrous.
Several attacks by the Chinese had succeeded in forcing
the Japanese to abandon the main gateway and retreat to
an interior defense posture within the palace building itself. At that point, the Japanese constructed a series of
walls, permitting them an easy retreat from one position
to another without making themselves vulnerable to attack. Thwarted on land, the Chinese went underground
and attempted to lay mines beneath the building by
digging tunnels and setting explosives. Despite such constant pressure, Shiba's units continued to hold the building.
Their tenacity was a major factor in their growing reputation as the pluckiest fighters in the foreign community.
Shiba himself earned increasing respect within the legation
quarter, and, had he been of higher rank (and a Caucasian),
he might have been entrusted with the overall command.

While the British and the Japanese were digging in
along Ch'ang An Street, the Russians and the Americans
were facing danger from another direction. By June 24
Chinese troops had begun to gather near the Ch'ien Men

along the south wall, a few hundred yards west of the legation defenses. That day a short surprise attack briefly
drove the American marines from their own cramped position on the wall above the American legation. For a short
period it appeared that the entire wall might have to be
abandoned. The defenders staged an immediate counter-
attack, however, and reoccupied their position. The ferocity of the struggle was illustrated in the American's treatment of their prisoners. All the Chinese troops seized
during the attack were bayoneted and thrown over the
wall. A young legation officer in charge of clearing the wall
labeled himself—with a lugubrious touch—the Major
General of the Corpses. To prevent a recurrence of the
attack, the Americans instructed Chinese coolies to bring
up more sandbags to strengthen the fortifications along the
wall.

By now the siege had been going on for nearly a
week. During that period the foreign community had been
exposed to constant firing from the Chinese side. By one
estimate, over a million shells landed in the legation area
during the first ten days of the siege. The foreign community's casualty list was growing. Many of the casualties
were directly attributable to the hostilities. Several people
were killed or wounded at the barricades, while others
were struck by random shells falling within the interior
lines of the compound. As might have been expected,
illness also exacted a growing toll. Sanitation problems
and inadequate diets contributed to a rising rate of dysentery, the only remedy for which was to drink a thin gruel
concocted of boiled water and rice.

By now any lingering sense of romance about the
siege had dissipated. The inherent dangers and the continued isolation from the outside world increased the anxiety of the defenders. Conditions within the compound
were rapidly deteriorating. The smells of war—the acrid
odor of gunpowder, the fetid stink of bloated corpses—
added to the normal pungent odors of a Chinese city in
summertime had become overpowering; many took to

The Ch'ien Men, at the center of the south wall of the Tartar city, Peking. This tower was burned by Boxers during the siege. (*Leslie's Weekly*, July 14, 1900, cover)

smoking cigars and cigarettes to gain relief from the
stench. Tempers were growing short, and, had not the
prospects of a massacre been ever-present, it is likely that
the defenders would have yielded to the pressure to
surrender.

Suddenly, on June 25, it seemed for a tantalizing
moment that the worst was over. Shortly after 4:00 P.M.
Chinese forces ceased firing and retreated from the barricades. A few minutes later a Chinese soldier appeared at
the North Bridge, at the juncture of Ch'ang An Street and
the Imperial Canal, with a signboard announcing a cease-
fire and declaring that a dispatch from the court would be
delivered to the ministers at the bridge. The ministers
agreed to the cease-fire and shortly before nightfall gathered
at the bridge to await the communication. The scene was
graphically described by Bertram Simpson:

The setting sun now struck the Imperial City, under whose orders
we had been so lustily bombarded, with a wonderful light. Just outside the Palace gates were crowds of Manchu and Chinese soldiery —
infantry, cavalry, and gunners grouped altogether in one mass of
colour. Never in my life have I seen such a wonderful panorama —
such a brilliant blaze in such rude and barbaric surroundings. There
were jackets and tunics of every colour; trouserings of blood-red
embroidered with black dragons; great two-handed swords in some
hands; men armed with bows and arrows mixing with Tung Fu-hsiang's
Kansu horsemen, who had the most modern carbines slung across
their backs. There were blue banners, yellow banners embroidered
with black, white and red flags, both triangular and square, all presented in a jumble to our wondering eyes. The Kansu soldiery of
Tung Fu-hsiang's command were easy to pick out from amongst
the milder looking Peking Banner troops. Tanned almost to the
colour of chocolate by years of campaigning in the sun, of sturdy
and muscular physique, these men who desired to be our butchers
showed by their aspect what little pity we should meet if they were
allowed to break in on us.[3]

The scene was obviously worthy of a great event. Ironically, it turned out to be a false alarm. No message arrived
from the other side, and shortly after nightfall the Chinese
troops resumed firing.

Not surprisingly, the besieged residents of the legation quarter interpreted this incident as another instance
of the unfathomable trickery of the Chinese, a diabolical
attempt to undermine the spirit of the foreigners by
raising—and then dashing—their hopes of survival. The
truth, apparently, was somewhat more complex. According to one source at court, the empress dowager had
decided to propose negotiations in a fit of pique at the
militant Prince Tuan. Earlier that day the latter, accompanied by Prince Chuang and other members of the
reactionary faction, had broken into the inner palace and
declared in tones of drunken bravado that they were going
to kill the *erh mao tzu,* the "second hairy one," meaning
the emperor. (In Chinese slang, Westerners were often
referred to as "hairy ones." A "second hairy one" was a
Chinese who supported the Westerners, usually a Christian
convert.) Tz'u Hsi had no particular love for her nephew,
who for a long time had been attempting in his ineffectual
manner to promote a conciliatory tone at court. But she
was a zealous defender of her own authority, and the
raucous demands of Prince Tuan and his cohorts aroused
her ire. To chastise them, she briefly favored the proposals
of the peace-minded Grand Secretary Jung Lu and prof-
fered the olive branch. When news of Chinese successes
against Seymour's allied expeditionary force at Lang Fang
reached the court later in the afternoon, her anger subsided and she ordered a resumption of attacks on the
legations. On such gossamer threads were sustained the
hopes of the besieged foreigners in Peking.

For the next few days with only desultory fighting,
neither side achieved any breakthroughs. The main problem for the legations during the final days of June was the
defense of the south wall, key to the entire defense effort.
Captain Jack Myers, commander of the U.S. Marine detachment on the wall, kept insisting that, with conditions
as they were, his men could no longer hold their positions
against any concerted attack. The heat, the constant
exposure to hostile gunfire, the cramped quarters, and the

Bird's-eye view of the top of the Tartar city wall, Peking. In the foreground is the Chinese barricade. The legation quarter is to the left. (*Leslie's Weekly*, August 18, 1900, p. 465)

lack of reinforcements made wall duty almost unbearable. It was only with difficulty that Sir Claude MacDonald convinced the Americans that there was no choice and persuaded them to stay.

Chinese probing along the south wall continued through June. On July 1 fierce Chinese attacks on the wall forced the Germans to withdraw from the barricade above their own legation, leaving the U.S. Marines nearby to abandon their positions. Fortunately, the attackers did not notice the retreat, and the defenders were able to return and strengthen the barricades against a possible recurrence.

Still, it was becoming increasingly obvious that the wall was the weakest link in the quarter's defense perimeter and the key to the survival of the legations. During the first week of July troops from the army of Tung Fu-hsiang began to build a serpentine brick wall which crept closer and closer to the American position on the wall. By the end of the week they were within twenty-five feet of the Americans. Since the approaching barricade was considerably higher than that of the Americans, the Chinese were moving toward a commanding position from which they could fire down onto the unprotected defenders.

When Captain Myers voiced his concern about this ominous new development, the ministers agreed that they would have to launch an attack to drive the Chinese back and dismantle the serpentine wall. At 3:00 A.M. on July 3 a mixed force of British, Russians, and Americans under the command of Captain Myers—slightly under fifty troops in all—made a surprise raid on the Chinese barricade. Two marines were killed in the attack and Myers himself was wounded in the leg, but the raid as a whole was a success. The Chinese, taken totally by surprise, retreated in disorder, leaving behind more than fifteen dead. After this incident the legation troops were able to hold their positions on the wall with little difficulty.

The length of the siege was taking its toll on the defenders, however. By June 27 thirty-two combat casualties, including eight fatalities, had been sustained in the

legation compound. A week later the casualty list had
grown to forty dead and seventy-two wounded. Adding to
the community's difficulties were the heat—the temperature frequently rose to over a hundred degrees in the shade—
and the debilitating effects of dysentery. Grumbling and
squabbling accompanied feats of heroism and resource-
fulness, and whole nationalities were frequently accused of
cowardice (usually the French and the Italians), lack of
discipline (usually the Americans), unwillingness to contri-
bute to the defense effort (most of the diplomatic community), and so on. Within the Chinese compound, the in-
cidence of smallpox and scarlet fever was on the rise,
adding to the continuing problems of sanitation, over-
crowding, and an inadequate diet.

On July 14 a second abortive effort to achieve a
cease-fire took place. The court once again seemed ready
to open negotiations and sent a message, allegedly drafted
by the moderate Prince Ch'ing, formerly head of the
Tsungli Yamen. The missive requested that the ministers
agree to leave the legation quarter under the protection of
Chinese military officers and take temporary refuge in the
Tsungli Yamen, a few blocks to the north. This move
would be undertaken, the message emphasized, "pending
future arrangements for your return home, in order to
preserve friendly relations intact from beginning to end."
It ended with a thinly veiled threat: "If no reply is received by the time fixed, even our affection will not
enable us to help you." The deadline for a reply was noon
the next day.

At this stage of the crisis the legations were not inclined to trust the intentions of the court. In their reply
the ministers emphasized that they were not convinced
that the Tsungli Yamen would be safer from attack than
their present location, perilous as the latter was. In response to the threat implied in the message, they stressed
that Chinese officials would be held fully responsible for
the deaths of any members of the foreign diplomatic
community.

The response from the Tsungli Yamen was surprisingly mild: since the preceding proposal was unacceptable to the foreign legations, the Tsungli Yamen would do its best to restrain the Boxers and maintain law and order in the capital. Appended to the message was a Chinese decree suspending hostilities indefinitely. In the remaining two weeks of July the level of fighting declined drastically, and an informal truce prevailed. With the firing stopped, life in the legations became marginally more comfortable. Also, they received the first definitive news of events in the outside world: an allied force had landed on the coast and was preparing to advance to Peking to relieve the siege. For the first time since mid-June, the foreigners in Peking felt that they might survive their ordeal.

Still, more than on anything else, survival depended on the attitude at court. Here the curious ambivalence displayed by the court toward the foreigners — the vacillation between a seemingly sincere concern for their welfare and an angry determination to punish them for their sins — was an accurate indication of the actual state of affairs in the imperial palace. The moderates continued their desperate efforts to restrain antiforeign sentiment. Jung Lu was convinced that the death of the foreigners would certainly spell the end of the dynasty, and he therefore made every effort to prevent a massacre. His troops took part in the siege, but, unlike those of Tung Fu-hsiang, they attempted to protect the foreigners from the Boxer attacks. The effort was difficult because, although the foreigners could as a rule distinguish between Jung Lu's troops and those of the Kansu army, they made little attempt to discriminate in their firing. To the foreigners, all Chinese outside the barricades were fair game.

In any event, Jung Lu's options were limited. To be too solicitous of the foreigners was dangerous and ran the risk of arousing the empress dowager's displeasure. Her hatred of the foreigners seemed unlimited, as witnessed by her frequent comment that she was resolved "to sleep on their skins and eat their flesh." The antiforeign mood still seemed to be dominant at court. If Ching-shan's *Diary* can be believed, even that aged court functionary seemed to share the enthusiasm, commenting that it was exciting to live in a time when foreigners' houses were burned, and when their decapitated heads could be seen hanging in a cage outside the palace gates. (The latter referred to the fate of Huberty James, a harmless European professor on the faculty at the Imperial Peking University. James, convinced that the Chinese could mean him no harm, wandered out into the streets of Peking early in the siege. He was captured, tortured, and put to death.) Under such conditions, if Jung Lu hoped to moderate the conflict, he would have to be extremely circumspect.

Yet the empress dowager had not committed herself irrevocably on the side of the militants and hesitated, irresolute, between the two factions. Most of the time she tended to lean strongly toward the hard-liners, and at one point she allegedly issued a decree directing that all foreigners be killed, without exception. Only the brave action of provincial officials, who refused to carry out the order, prevented a general massacre.[4] At the same time she was capable of acting with almost ludicrous generosity under the circumstances—in early July she had ordered Prince Ch'ing to present the besieged foreigners with gifts of fresh fruit as a gesture of good will from the court.

For decades historians have puzzled over the character of this enigmatic woman.[5] Tz'u Hsi was, in fact, being pulled violently in different ways, not only by the squabbling factions at court, but by forces in the recesses of her own psyche. For reasons that have never been satisfactorily explained, she had hated foreigners all her life. She apparently felt the greatest resentment toward missionaries. By what right, she would often exclaim to her confidants, does the barbarian come here to teach us religion? She was, by all accounts, an immensely practical woman and capable of dissembling her true feelings. She had done so a few days before the siege began when she invited the ladies of the diplomatic community to attend a reception and murmured over and over, "All one family, all one family." Yet, according to intimates, she had a strong belief in the occult and was receptive to the claims of the Boxers that they could protect her dynasty from the depredations of the foreigner.

More than instinctively disliking foreigners, Tz'u Hsi firmly believed that they wished to oust her from power and replace her with Kuang Hsü. From her early years at court, she had possessed a virtually maniacal ambition to rise to power, and, when she felt thwarted, her revenge was limitless. It is possible that the impetus for the Boxer crisis was the emperor's *coup d'etat* of 1898 and Tz'u Hsi's belief that Kuang Hsü was encouraged in his actions by outside powers. Her anger at the foreigners' alleged interference in China's internal affairs was never assuaged, and it seems that all the delicate diplomacy of the powers—including the careful distinction they made between war and a police action—in her case fell on deaf ears. Tz'u Hsi had persuaded herself that all foreigners were a threat to her own security—and thus to the survival of the dynasty—and it is possible that only military defeat prevented her from carrying out her wish to punish their representatives in Peking. Yet she always seemed to hold back from the brink and never seemed to question the failure of the Chinese forces to breach the defenses of the legations. The practical statesman, at last resort, seemed to predominate over the unreasoning patriot. While Tz'u Hsi struggled with her emotions, the fate of the foreign community hung in the balance.

Throughout the crisis Jung Lu served as a major restraining force on the militants at court. Although he frequently complained to foreign visitors that it was sheer suicide to be too proforeign in the wolves' den of the court, he persistently used his influence to keep the foreigners alive. He withheld from Tung Fu-hsiang the use of several new Krupp cannons, the employment of which would have reduced the legation quarter to rubble in a few hours. This constraint led the Muslim general to accuse Jung Lu of betraying the dynasty.

Jung Lu warned Tz'u Hsi of the danger of further alienating the great powers and beseeched her not to risk the empire "on a single throw of the dice." He told her that the Boxers had grown too powerful, that the dynasty was like an animal whose tail is too large (this was a particularly persuasive argument, since the empress dowager was almost paranoid in matters affecting her authority). And, whenever possible, he turned the mistakes of his rivals into advantages, as when he disclosed the fact that Prince Tuan had concocted the forged ultimatum demanding her resignation. It was the sweet reasonableness of Jung Lu's arguments that prevailed on Tz'u Hsi to decree on July 17 that the level of hostilities be reduced. On the same day she dispatched letters to Berlin, Paris, and Washington, asking these governments to help resolve the crisis and assuring them that the diplomats and their families in Peking were alive and well.

Through the last two weeks of July, as the uneasy truce prevailed, envoys from the legations informed the court that the defending forces were withholding their fire unless fired upon. Soldiers on both sides strolled on the barricades and fraternized. Some foreign troops even took snapshots of their Chinese counterparts. During the lull negotiations continued sporadically at several levels. The court was increasingly concerned at the possible consequences of a head-on confrontation in Peking, but it seemed unable to control the Boxers; as a compromise it concentrated its efforts on getting the foreigners out of the capital. Faced with the refusal of the envoys to move to the Tsungli Yamen, it now renewed its offer to escort the foreign community to Tientsin, nearer the coast. If the foreigners still refused to leave, the court repeated, it could not be held responsible for the consequences.

The ministers, however, were still not persuaded. They suspected, not unreasonably, that the offer might be a ruse to lure them from behind the barricades into an exposed position where they could be attacked. Moreover, they reasoned, if we are not safe in Peking, why would we be more secure in Tientsin, which had itself been under attack since early summer? Minister Conger, in particular, felt strongly about remaining in the legation quarter and wired Secretary Hay that any move from the safety of the barricades meant "certain death" for the foreigners.

The court was not dissuaded by the suspicion and reluctance in the legation quarter and pursued its argument in messages to the powers. The court assured them that their envoys within the legation quarter were safe and in comfortable surroundings and asked the powers to assist the Chinese government in evacuating their representatives from the capital to Tientsin. The reaction in world capitals to the dynasty's pleas was not significantly different from that of the envoys in Peking. Though not as conscious as the diplomatic community in China of the mixed messages emanating from the court, the governments of the powers were generally firm in their attitudes toward a solution of the conflict. Negotiations were to proceed through the accredited envoys in Peking, and no agreement could be reached until and unless the safety of such representatives was assured. To achieve such conditions, the powers informed China by various means that the only solution was for the Chinese government to cooperate with the allied expedition attempting to reach Peking to relieve the legations.

As the month of July neared its end, then, the court appeared to be seeking a way out. Within the court, however, the controversy over policy continued unabated, and some paid with their lives. On July 22 two members of the moderate factions—Hsü Ching-ch'eng, a former diplomat and head of the Imperial University of Peking, and Yüan Ch'ang, an official in the Tsungli Yamen—had submitted a memorial to the throne that was critical of the Boxers. For their pains they were decapitated. This sudden expression of militancy was probably a direct re-

sult of the arrival at court of Li Ping-heng, the deposed
governor of Shantung. In the interval since his degrada-
tion at the behest of the Germans he had been appointed
high commissioner in command of the imperial naval
forces in the Yangtse area—despite the court's earlier
promise to the great powers that he would henceforth be
ineligible for high office. In early June he was offered the
viceroyship of Chihli. He tried to refuse, but without success, and was ordered to Tientsin immediately.

It was soon evident that Li's hatred of foreigners
was as virulent as ever. He arrived at court on July 22 and
immediately began to play on the empress dowager's
antiforeign feelings while simultaneously planning new
attacks on the legations with Prince Tuan. It was presumably his intervention which sealed the doom of the
two moderates. Li was a very strong-minded individual,
and it is an indication of his influence on Tz'u Hsi that he
was promptly appointed joint commander, with the
moderate Jung Lu, of all Chinese armed forces in the capital area. The Chinese leader with the strongest antiforeign
feelings of all now held four armies under his command.

For a few days Li's presence had no effect on the
general situation. Negotiations continued, and as late as
July 27 the court sent a gift of rice and melons to the legations. But the new tough mood at court could not long be
denied, and it soon broke into the open. On July 29 the
Chinese troops surrounding the legation quarter reopened
hostilities. From that day until the end of the siege their
attacks would intensify, leading many of the foreigners
to lose hope that they would be saved.

Chapter Seven

The Battle of Tientsin

Peking was not the only Chinese city to be exposed to the bitter struggle between East and West. The commercial city of Tientsin, halfway between the capital and the coast, had a large foreign population, mostly merchants and consular officials. The foreigners resided in a large concession area on the south bank of the Pei Ho at the east end of the city. Unlike Peking, Tientsin had been the scene of several antiforeign riots throughout recent history. In 1870 a crowd of angry Chinese had attacked a French church and orphanage in the heart of the city. The orphanage was looted, and the French priests and nuns on the premises were massacred. Also, the French Catholic cathedral, Notre Dame des Victoires, the most prominent symbol of the Western presence in north China, was burned to the ground.

In the early summer of 1900 the foreign concession area suddenly experienced an influx of frightened Western missionaries and railway employees fleeing from rampaging Boxer gangs operating throughout the provinces of north China. By mid-June Boxers had entered the native city in force, looting and burning. Several Chinese suspected of

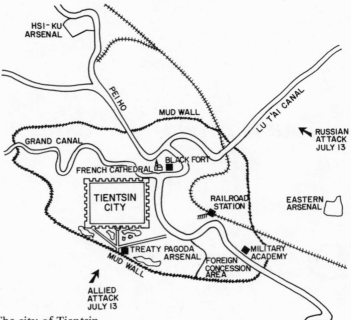

The city of Tientsin

harboring sympathies for the foreigners were killed. The local government, apparently unwilling to antagonize the rioters, took no action.

Faced with the growing threat of violence, the foreign community in Tientsin began to look to its defenses. In some respects, the foreign position seemed more secure here than in Peking, for within the metropolitan area there were over two thousand foreign troops, including seventeen hundred Russians and 560 seamen of mixed nationality who had been dispatched from the foreign ships along the coast at Taku. Then, too, Tientsin was nearer the coast and theoretically more accessible to foreign military action. In other ways, however, the position of the foreigners in Tientsin was less favorable. The Western troops in the area were poorly armed, since most of the heavy artillery had been sent upriver with Admiral Seymour's expeditionary force.

Also, the foreign concession area in Tientsin was in some respects more vulnerable to attack than its counterpart in Peking. It did not have the advantage of the massive city wall at its rear. Tientsin was surrounded by a ten-foot-high earthen rampart which encircled not only the Chinese city and the concession area but many of the suburban villages as well. The foreign settlement was situated between the city wall on the south and the river, the Pei Ho, on the north. Considerably larger than the legation quarter in Peking—well over a mile in length and several hundred yards in width at its widest—it was much harder to defend. Because of the shortage of arms, the defenders could only station one rifleman for every hundred yards at some points along the perimeter.

Moreover, the area was more open to outside attack, particularly on the west. The streets ran perpendicular and at right angles to the river, so that Chinese troops on the north bank had an easy line of fire into the heart of the settlement. The situation was made even more dangerous by the presence of several hundred Chinese Christians huddled for protection within the concession area. Because this group could be easily infiltrated from the outside, the danger of sniper fire from the hostile forces *within* the enclosed area was ever present. Most of the foreigners gathered in the cellar of the municipal hall in the English settlement, protected by earthworks and bales of cotton. The Americans were housed in the compound of the commissioner of customs, near the center of the settlement and surrounded by Chinese godowns. All the Chinese were located in the compound of a mining company across the street.

If the layout of their area was not as favorable to the defenders as in Peking, the foreigners in Tientsin seemed more organized and more willing to work for their own survival. Unlike their counterparts in the capital city, the residents, civilian as well as military, appeared willing to perform even the most menial tasks in the interests of survival. The first priority, of course, was to establish a line of defense. Here, as in Peking, the defenders began constructing barricades, particularly along the west end, where the settlement adjoined the eastern suburbs of the Chinese city. The work was supervised by a capable young American mining engineer who would later become president of the United States—Herbert Hoover.

Hoover set the tone for the besieged community. He was a dynamo of energy—supervising the defenses, leading a squad of British infantry outside the compound each night to obtain water from the boilers of the nearby municipal water plant, caring for the Chinese converts within the concession area. (At one point he had to rescue several from execution by a group of foreigners convinced that many of the Chinese in the settlement were actually working for the Chinese forces outside).[1] Hoover's wife, Lou, was equally helpful, serving as a volunteer nurse in the settlement's hospital.

Beyond the Tientsin barricades were about five thousand imperial Chinese troops, mostly members of the Front Army of General Nieh Shih-ch'eng, supplemented by at least twenty-five thousand Boxers. Better armed than their Western adversaries, they possessed some heavy artillery pieces. These were placed at the governor-general's yamen in the heart of the Chinese city and along the western bank of the Lu T'ai Canal, which ran from the city in a generally northeasterly direction toward Tangshan. Had they been good marksmen, the Chinese could have leveled the defenses of the foreign settlement in a matter of days. According to contemporary reports, however, they had not been adequately trained in the use of their new weapons. As a result, their firing was haphazard and did little damage. Not one fatality due to shelling was reported throughout the entire siege.

The first concerted assaults on the foreigners in Tientsin occurred on June 15, when Chinese troops attacked the city railway station, across the river and to the northwest of the concession area. Under normal circumstances, this station would have been outside the perimeter of the foreign defense line, and its loss would have deprived the defenders of their sole link to the coast. At the precise moment when the attack took place, however, seventeen hundred Russian troops were at the station preparing to leave by rail to join Seymour's beleaguered force upriver toward the capital. They repelled the initial Chinese attack and, as one writer on the period pointed out, not only preserved the station for possible future use, but also provided a much needed tonic for the morale of the Tientsin foreign community. For the remainder of the siege, the railway station became a symbol of the foreigners' link to the outside world.

In succeeding days the intensity of the Chinese attacks increased. Most were focused on the western edge of the concession area. The narrow streets and Chinese houses just beyond the foreign defense line at this point provided useful cover for advancing Chinese troops. The Chinese also made use of their heavy artillery, causing considerable damage to the buildings in the concession area. Ironically, the allied attack on the Taku forts heightened the danger in the foreign settlement. Chinese units retreating from the coast gathered in the Tientsin area and reinforced the troops already there.

For the next few days the allied forces were generally compelled to remain on the defensive. Within the obvious limits of their capabilities, however, they did attempt to take the offensive. Their first target was a Chinese military school directly across the river from the concession area. They intended to put out of action several Chinese artillery pieces that had been doing extensive damage to the allied defenses. The attack was successful, but an attempt to dispatch troops upriver to relieve Seymour's stranded force failed.

Until help arrived the foreign community could do little except dig in. There was some discussion of attempting to fight back to the coast, but the proposal was rejected out of fear of further isolating the legations in Peking. The key, then, was to obtain assistance from the allied forces at Taku. At the beginning of the siege the allied authorities at Tientsin had sent several hundred of their precious troops—Germans, French, and Russians—down the line toward the coast to protect the track from sabotage by Boxers. The railway was the allies' only link with the coast, because the Pei Ho was too shallow in summer to permit regular river traffic. Now, however, the entire area between Tientsin and Taku was filled with imperial troops and roaming bands of Boxers. On June 19 the foreigners in Tientsin sent messengers down toward the coast in an attempt to let the allied naval commanders at Taku know of their perilous situation. The messages urged the allied forces to advance to Tientsin at the earliest opportunity to relieve the defenders.

Since their seizure of the Taku forts, the allied commanders had tried to avoid antagonizing the Chinese government and had issued a statement assuring local officials of their peaceful intentions. When they learned of the critical situation of the foreigners at Tientsin, however, the commanders made immediate plans to send a relieving column to the rescue. On the same day, June 20, a small mixed force, including a battalion of the 1st Regiment of the U.S. Marines under Major Littleton Waller, began to move inland from the coast. The small complement of 7 officers and 132 enlisted men was reinforced by 30 additional troops from the *U.S.S. Nashville.* (The ship had landed at Taku on June 19.) The men traveled three miles upriver to the rail hub at Tangku where they learned they were to break through to Tientsin, thirty miles away.

The relief force moved out from Tangku early on June 20. Major Waller had decided to follow the railbed up toward Tientsin in order to clear the line for later reinforcements. Boxers had torn out many of the rails, however, so Waller's small force had to repair the lines as they advanced. They met little organized resistance and made fairly rapid progress through the flat, treeless plain. By nightfall they had reached a point about twelve miles from Tientsin, where they encountered a force of several hundred Russian troops. Waller wanted to bivouac for the night, since reinforcements were expected the next day, but the Russian commander decided on an immediate advance. Reluctantly, Waller consented to accompany him with his own forces. Meeting no opposition, the joint force arrived at the imperial arsenal, a few miles northeast of the city, just before dawn. Here for the first time they ran into a mixed force of two thousand regular troops and a larger number of Boxers. After a brief exchange of fire, the allies were forced to retire and wait for reinforcements.

The advance of the small Russian and American contingent relieved pressure on the foreign settlement by compelling Chinese military units in the area to face the new allied threat from the east. On the following day the Russo-American contingent was bolstered by the arrival from Taku of a larger mixed force, consisting of several hundred Germans, Italians, and Japanese, four hundred British, and about fifteen hundred Russians. Unlike Waller's marines, this force had encountered severe resistance along the way. The price that the local population paid for this resistance was graphically described by George Lynch, a British journalist who traveled from Tangku to Tientsin by rail a few days later:

> Here one got the first touch of that feeling which intensified as we advanced—a palpable breath of blasting desolation that seemed to have passed over the land. It was a strange feeling passing through what had evidently been a densely populated country, but what was now the scene of tenantless houses, often roofless, frequently with charred walls, empty doors and windows, that gave them a skull-like appearance to the imagination.
>
> The train proceeded slowly with frequent stoppages. It was midday before we reached the railway station at Tientsin.
>
> I think it would have been very difficult in the annals of warfare to find a picture parallel to that which the railway presented. Every roof and wall was riddled with shot and shell. The boilers of the locomotives which were inside the railway shed were simply perforated like sieves, trucks and carriages were derailed, and the plaster of the walls of the shed just pock-marked with bullets.[2]

The second force joined the American and Russian units on the morning of June 22 and marched into the foreign concession area unopposed. At least temporarily, the siege was lifted.

For the next few days the situation at Tientsin looked brighter. Women and children were evacuated by rail to the coast. New allied units arrived continually, including four companies of Russians and a company of the Welsh Fusiliers. The first action of the growing allied force was to relieve Seymour's units, still under constant Boxer attack at Peitsang. On June 26 Seymour's battered force returned to Tientsin, sixteen days after its original departure for Peking. In two weeks of constant harassment, 12 men had been killed and over 250 wounded.

The arrival of the allied reinforcements relieved the situation in Tientsin and forced the imperial troops and Boxer units in the area to retreat temporarily from the immediate vicinity of the foreign community. But the danger was hardly over. The allied forces at Tientsin now totaled over twelve thousand troops of various nationalities, and their firepower was considerably strengthened by the addition of six Krupp cannons. The Chinese were also increasing their numbers; they now had eighty thousand regulars supplemented by an estimated three hundred thousand Boxers. Thus the troops who had arrived to relieve the defenders found themselves besieged.

In defiance of the odds, the allies were determined to take the offensive. In the early morning of June 27 a Russian force located on the northern bank of the river, directly across from the foreign settlement, launched a successful assault on the Chinese military arsenal about five miles northeast of the city. The attack was not easy. The Russians were forced to advance across an open plain against a well-armed fort surrounded by a moat and manned by over a thousand Chinese troops. The first attack was met with heavy fire, resulting in several hundred casualties. The Russians appealed for reinforcements, and at 10:00 A.M. a mixed Anglo-American force of eight hundred men advanced to join the Russians, now pinned down behind the embankment of the Tangku-Tientsin railway. With fire from the arsenal still heavy, and a strong force of Chinese camped on the plain just to the south, the allies decided on a heavy bombardment. The assault blew up the arsenal's magazine and caused a retreat of the occupants; the allies occupied the arsenal with no further opposition. With this attack they had cleared all the Chinese troops from the area across the Pei Ho from the foreign settlement. The main body of Chinese forces was still located along the bank of the Lu T'ai Canal and to the west and southwest of the native city.

For several days both sides restricted their activities to a few cautious sorties. But on July 6, encouraged by allied inactivity, Ma Yü-k'un, the new commander of the Left Army, called for an advance, taking advantage of his superiority in numbers and firepower. Over a period of several days the Chinese gradually extended their lines to the north and southwest of the foreign defenses, with their left flank at the juncture of the mud wall and the Lu T'ai Canal, and extending southwest to a point beyond the western edge of Tientsin. From there they continued their heavy bombardment on the foreign settlement.

The heaviest attacks fell on the westernmost allied position—a British battery on the mud wall at the west end of the foreign settlement. To reduce the pressure on the British position, a force of two thousand troops, mostly Japanese but reinforced by U.S. Marines, launched an assault on the source of the bombardment—the Western arsenal, directly south of the native city. (This was also known as the Treaty Pagoda Arsenal, because the Treaty of Tientsin had been signed there in 1860.) The successful attack was undertaken by means of a flanking movement to the southwest and the northeast. The seizure of the arsenal not only reduced the shelling from that area on the foreign settlement but also cleared the area south of the city and west of the concession area of Chinese troops, thus temporarily eliminating the danger of encirclement.

In the meantime, there was also fighting on the northern front. The Chinese, apparently wary of the allied defenses, had shied away from a direct confrontation. But on July 11 Chinese forces attacked Russian positions on the north bank of the river along the railway line. They were driven back, but the allied forces suffered heavy casualties.

This skirmishing, however, was only a prelude to the main event. Throughout the early part of July the allied commanders were making plans for a concerted two-pronged assault on Chinese defenses along the Lu T'ai Canal and surrounding the native city.[3] The attack on the canal to the north would be led by Russian and German troops already located on the plain north of the Pei Ho. The remaining forces—Japanese, French, British, American, and Austrian—would launch an assault on the native city from the south.

The assault on the city presented a number of problems. Like the capital, the city of Tientsin was surrounded by a wall of earth and brick twenty-two feet high and about sixteen feet wide. With sizable contingents of Chinese regulars to the north and west, the only feasible point of attack was from the south, where allied units had already cleared Chinese forces in their attack on the Treaty Pagoda Arsenal. The terrain was not particularly favorable for an assault, however. The allied units would have to cross the mud wall at the point of the arsenal and then advance about fifteen hundred yards across a low plain to the city wall. This plain was pockmarked with pools and ditches, and its several tiny villages offered ideal cover for bands of Chinese snipers bent on harassing the advancing allies. Moreover, throughout the advance the attackers would be exposed to enemy fire from the top of the city wall directly ahead.

The most logical point for an assault on the city wall was at the southwestern corner; there the allied units would be less exposed to fire from the wall. But the Chinese had flooded the canal just beyond the wall at that point, making it impossible for the allies to deploy troops in sufficient numbers to launch an effective assault. The attack would have to be made from the south, aiming directly at the main gate to the city in the center of the south wall. Once allied forces had traversed the moat and reached the wall just beyond it, Japanese sappers would blow up the south gate of the city. The remaining allied forces would enter the city and rout the defenders. Between the allied force—some five thousand strong—and their objective were an estimated fifty thousand Chinese troops.

Shortly after midnight on the morning of July 13 the allied units began to take their positions in preparation for the assault on Tientsin. The Japanese, some fifteen hundred men in all, would occupy the center. They were commanded by Major General Yasumasa Fukushima, the highest ranking allied military officer in Tientsin. To their right would be nine hundred French troops under Colonel de Pelicot, while the British, commanded by General F. R. Dorward, would be to the left of the Japanese troops. Also under Dorward's command would be a small contingent of Austrians and two American regiments—the 9th Infantry commanded by Colonel Emerson Liscum and a regiment of the 1st Marines under Colonel Robert L. Meade.

By dawn the attacking force had begun to cross the mud wall near the Treaty Pagoda Arsenal. The arsenal itself presented no problem, because it had been held since the ninth by a small allied force posted there to keep the Chinese from reoccupying the area. Once across the mud wall, however, the attacking force began to run into difficulties. The ground between the wall and the native city was uneven, forcing the Japanese in the center to advance along a raised road which led directly north toward the south gate of the city. Heavy fire from the Chinese soon compelled the Japanese to seek cover, but there was little shelter in the fields alongside the road. The problem was increased by the fact that the Chinese, to impede a possible allied attack, had flooded the area by diverting water from several nearby canals. The attackers found themselves

in an open plain, exposed to heavy fire, and with many of
their number standing knee-deep in water and mud. To
make matters worse, a large force of Chinese regulars was
located a few thousand yards beyond the left flank of the
allied force. Were they to attack, the entire operation
would be in serious jeopardy.

At this point the confusion of coalition command
led to disaster. Since the American units had no general,
they had been placed under the ultimate command of the
British general, Dorward. Colonel Meade, the highest
ranking American officer at Tientsin, had not been invited
to attend the strategy meeting of the allied commanders
and was simply informed of the decisions made at the
meeting. Perhaps for this reason, the American units did
not have a specific responsibility in the attack on Tientsin
but were merely given the vague order to support the
Japanese, the main force attacking in the center. When
General Dorward ordered all units under his command to
move up to support the Japanese, who had become bogged
down in their advance toward the south gate, Colonel
Liscum, commanding officer of the three hundred enlisted
men and eighteen officers of the 9th Infantry, requested
specific orders from the general. The latter simply informed Liscum that it did not matter whether he advanced
to the right or left of the Japanese, as long as his men were
able to find cover.

How Liscum interpreted this remark will never be
known. It is possible that in the confusion of the battle
he lost his bearings. In any event, after crossing the mud
wall on the left of the Japanese, instead of advancing
directly toward the south gate under the shelter of the
raised road, the men of the 9th Infantry crossed the road
and moved to the right, along a road which moved almost
at right angles to the front and in the general direction of
the concession area. By doing so they exposed themselves
to a merciless fire from the Chinese on the city wall and in
the villages between the native city and the advancing
allies. The Americans sought cover, but there was little

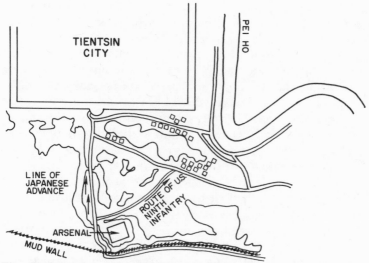

The allied attack on Tientsin, July 13, 1900

protection save a few small mounds and gravestones.[4] Pinned down by the heavy fire, they took heavy losses — seventeen were killed (including Colonel Liscum) and seventy-one wounded. Once their perilous position became obvious, General Dorward attempted to relieve them, but without success. The badly battered Americans were forced to dig in and finally made their retreat to the Treaty Pagoda Arsenal at nightfall.

While Liscum's force was being decimated by Chinese fire to the right of the main force, the two battalions of the 1st Marine regiment under Major Waller to the left of the main advancing force were themselves pinned down in the flooded fields about three hundred yards from the city wall. Fortunately, they were able to find shelter behind low mud walls, where they waited for the Japanese to break through to the wall.

While the Americans blundered about in the flooded fields to either side of the raised roadway, the Japanese waited until the murderous fire from the city slackened and then recommenced their gradual advance. By the end of the day they had reached a position near the city wall from which they would be able to open an attack on the city gate the following morning.

At 3:00 A.M. on July 14 the allies renewed their assault on Tientsin. Japanese demolition units forced their way across the city moat and, after considerable difficulty, managed to set a charge which blew up the outer entrance to the south gate. The first attempt to detonate the charge electrically failed when a Chinese bullet cut the wire leading to the charge. Finally, a young Japanese officer braved the fusillade, rushed forward, and managed to light the fuse with a match. After the spectacular explosion the Japanese infantry rushed through the gate and found that the Chinese defenders had fled in disarray. They also discovered, however, that they were now in an inner court-yard and blocked from further advance by a second gate leading into the city. One resourceful soldier scaled the wall and opened the second gate from the inside. The Japanese entered Tientsin and found that the Chinese had abandoned the city.

The allies had succeeded, but with considerable losses — 750 casualties out of a total force of slightly over 5,000. The Japanese had borne the brunt of the fighting and over 300 of their men had been killed or wounded. Casualties of the American units, including Colonel Liscum's 9th Infantry, were 24 dead and 98 wounded. By allied estimates, the Chinese had suffered over 5,000 casualties.

While the allied forces were clinging to their positions in the muddy flatlands south of the native city, the Russian and German units to the north were having an easier time advancing against Chinese batteries at the Blackfort. This Chinese defense position was located near the burned Catholic cathedral at the junction of the Grand Canal and the Pei Ho and on the west bank of the Lu T'ai Canal. Meeting little resistance, the allied forces advanced steadily toward the Chinese positions. Before day's end they had taken the Chinese batteries along the canal and pushed on to seize two Chinese camps in the vicinity.

By nightfall they had returned to the allied camp with only 150 men killed or wounded.

With the battle over, the allies imposed harsh punishment. This was part of the turn-of-the-century psychology of war. Chastising the defeated city like a misbehaving child was considered the best means of teaching the enemy the wages of sin. Opening the city to looting and burning would teach the Chinese the folly of waging war against the powers. Tientsin was doubly unfortunate, for shortly after the allied victory a rumor spread throughout the Western capitals that the defenses of the legations in Peking had been breached and the entire foreign community massacred. This news—apparently spread by a staffer of the London *Daily Mail* in Shanghai—was generally accepted as true and was reported by many Western papers in lurid detail. A memorial service for the dead was actually scheduled at St. Paul's Cathedral in London, and hundreds of families throughout the world mourned the loss of their loved ones.

It did not take long to discover that the rumor was a hoax and that the legations were still holding their ground at the capital. Nevertheless, the news of the massacre undoubtedly affected the behavior of the allied troops in Tientsin. In the erroneous belief that the legations had fallen, the allied force occupying Tientsin engaged in an orgy of looting. But to say that they destroyed a living city would be an overstatement. The retreating Chinese forces, for reasons of their own, had already looted and burned before their departure. Now the occupying troops made their own contribution and plundered the city at will until they exhausted themselves.

A good example of world reaction to the ravaging of Tientsin came from British correspondent Henry Savage Landor, whose *China and the Allies* soon became one of the standard works on the war. "It certainly seemed a pity," he wrote, "to let so much beautiful and valuable property be wasted. Was it not, then, the lesser evil to allow these men, who had fought hard, to reap what benefit they could from the misfortune of others, especially since 'the others' were doomed to misfortune in any case?" As for the justice of punishing the innocent for the sins of the guilty, Landor observed, "It was the only way by which the natives could be punished for their outrages on our men, women and children; and, degrading as it may seem to those who had no chance of taking part in it, there is no doubt that the only portion of this war which will cause the Chinese some future reflection will be the burning and looting of Tientsin."[5]

Once the destructive instincts of the allied troops subsided, the foreign commanders started imposing law and order in the conquered city. Tientsin was partitioned into four sectors assigned to Great Britain, France, Japan, and the United States. A three-man council was formed to act as a provisional government; it had full powers of policing, taxation, and the maintenance of law and order. As a grim footnote to the fate of the city, Chinese coolies were paid twenty cents a day to bury the dead.

THE REACTION AT COURT

The fall of Tientsin had several beneficial consequences for the allied forces. In the first place, it cleared the way for a possible advance to Peking and the relief of the legations. Secondly, the sizable contingents of allied forces that were placed within a few miles of the capital reduced the danger of a Chinese attack on other centers of western influence in central and southern China. Finally, the defeat of the city had a tangible effect on the court in Peking. By graphically demonstrating the weakness of Chinese defenses, it forced the government to begin thinking the unthinkable—that they themselves might suffer defeat. For several weeks the empress dowager and many of her advisers had been persuaded that the Boxers, if not precisely invulnerable to Western bullets, at least symbolized the will of the people, their tenacious loyalty to the dynasty, and their growing anger at the depredations of the foreigners in China. While making conciliatory gestures to Western capitals in the hopes of arresting their advance toward the capital, the empress dowager had apparently cherished the secret hope that her troops, aided by "her children," could really save China from foreign conquest. For a while the news from the front had been fairly encouraging. Governor-general Yü Lu had reported several victories for Chinese forces under Generals Nieh Shih-ch'eng and Ma Yü-k'un over allied units, thus allowing the court to believe optimistically that the foreign powers could be driven from the area of Tientsin.

Unfortunately for China, the situation was not as rosy as it seemed through the reports sent by Yü Lu. Within the Chinese camp there had been little cooperation and much friction between General Nieh and the Boxers. Since early June the general had displayed contempt for the Boxers and had made every effort to disperse them from the capital area and along the railway from Peking to the coast. In fact, Nieh's actions against the Boxers became so open that he was reproved by the court and ordered to treat them with more restraint. Throughout the month of June, however, he had continued to suppress Boxer activities in the area between Tientsin and the capital, claiming that his actions were necessary to protect the railway and thus prevent the advance of foreign troops. In early July the empress dowager had ordered him dismissed from office, but before the command could be carried out General Nieh had deliberately put himself in the line of fire and died on the battlefield a few days before the final allied attack on Tientsin. Nevertheless, the death of their foremost enemy did not result in a better performance by the Boxers in the struggle against the powers. As pressure on Tientsin mounted, the Boxers melted away; they were of little assistance during the final attack on the city. The tenacious myth of the Boxers—which for several weeks had alternately thrilled and terrorized so many—was now effectively destroyed.

On hearing of the fall of Tientsin, Prince Tuan had

assured Tz'u Hsi that Chinese forces, aided by the Boxers, would be able to protect the capital. Now, as the reputation of the Boxers became tarnished, the mood at court grew more pessimistic. This pessimism intensified when messages were received from the viceroys in central and south China appealing to the court to negotiate a solution to the crisis. One memorial, sent on the day following the allied victory at Tientsin, asked the court to offer protection to foreign residents in China and compensation for damages sustained during the conflict. It also proposed that the court issue a decree announcing explicitly that all riotous elements in China would be vigorously suppressed and that letters be sent to France and the United States asking for help in ending the crisis.

The court, in reaction to the events that were taking place around Tientsin, wasted no time in complying with some of the requests. It sent letters to the heads of state of France, Germany, and the United States, reassuring them that their diplomatic representatives in China were secure and in good health. It reiterated its proposal to provide safe conduct for the envoys and their families out of Peking. It directed the Tsungli Yamen to promise that it would do all in its power to prevent rioting elements in Peking from attacking the foreign community. Finally, in an apparent gesture of good faith, it announced a new cease-fire.

As we have seen, however, the court's gestures of conciliation would prove to be temporary and would soon be succeeded by a new attitude of toughness. The arrival of Li Ping-heng in Peking emboldened Tz'u Hsi and the militants, and the advocates of peace were terrorized into silence by the execution of Hsü Ching-ch'eng and Yüan Ch'ang. Once again the gods of war ruled in Peking.

Chapter Eight

The Advance to Peking

F or several weeks the court had vacillated between peace and war. Within the palace walls the militants appeared to have the upper hand, with only Jung Lu strong enough to balance the reactionaries' influence on the empress dowager. Jung Lu's major allies were not in Peking, but in central and south China, where the viceroys were doing their best to defuse the crisis. However, Li Hung-chang, Liu K'un-yi, and Chang Chih-tung were not in total agreement on how to deal with the situation. Chang, in particular, appeared somewhat timorous about taking a strong stand, perhaps in fear of antagonizing the Manchu aristocracy at court. The viceroys were at one, however, in hoping that negotiations could begin before the allies began their final advance to Peking, a move that they felt could spell disaster for the dynasty.

Most prominent in pursuit of peace was the aged statesman Li Hung-chang. Appointed viceroy of Chihli on July 13 — the day the allies attacked Tientsin — Li was reluctant to leave for the north without a clear understanding of the rapidly changing situation. While still in Canton he consulted with representatives of the great powers. He promised to remain neutral if the allies agreed

Chinese plenipotentiary Li Hung-chang in a sedan chair (*Harper's Weekly,* November 24, 1900, cover)

to respect the person of the empress dowager, and he informed them that he was hopeful of setting up negotiations between the two sides at Tientsin, since a meeting in Peking at that time seemed out of the question. The allies were not ready to acquiesce, however, and replied that negotiations would have to take place with the duly appointed representatives in Peking or—in case of their deaths—with the governments of the great powers themselves.

Li realized that the positions of the two sides were irreconcilable. China would not negotiate while under attack; on the other hand, to allow the conflict to continue risked occupation of the capital city by the great powers. To Li the only reasonable solution was to arrange for the evacuation of the foreign community from Peking to Tientsin. Short of that, Li wished to see at least a cease-fire agreement reached so that negotiations could get under way. The foreigners, however, refused to leave, and their home governments would not open negotiations with China unless the safety of their envoys had been adequately demonstrated. The only way the safety of the foreign community could be assured, in their view, was for the court to permit the peaceful entry of the allied expeditionary force into Peking to rescue their fellow countrymen.

Li's views were reported in a brief but explicit telegram to the Department of State from the American consul at Shanghai:

Saw Li as directed. Says purpose attempt persuade Throne send ministers Tientsin. Afterwards hopes military operations will be suspended; then negotiations can follow. Says Boxers and troops can be stopped by Chinese Government. Asks is it possible, if ministers are escorted Tientsin safely, that military operations can be suspended? Assures ministers now safe.[1]

Li placed great hope in the effect of the conciliatory attitude on the United States, whom he viewed as the least hostile of the great powers involved in the conflict. He may have been right in this assessment, for Secretary of State Hay had informed the French ambassador that he wanted to be responsive to the moderate messages emanating from various sources in China. But when Li appealed to Washington Hay responded that negotiations could not begin before communications were allowed to resume between the powers and their diplomatic representatives in Peking. Li, contending that if the powers attacked Peking the foreigners there would all be killed, asked Hay whether the allied advance would be stopped if such communications were established. Hay replied that it would not be expedient at that time to submit the proposal to the other allied powers. Instead, he suggested that Li advise the Chinese authorities "to place themselves in friendly communication and cooperation with the relief expedition," and to put the allied governments in contact with their own diplomatic representatives in Peking. Otherwise, he warned, the court would be assuming "a heavy responsibility."

Hay was taking a firm line with Li, but throughout the month of July he had himself been searching for ways to defuse the crisis. On receiving a plea from the viceroys in central China that the powers refrain from sending forces into the Yangtse Valley area, Hay replied that the United States had no intention of sending forces to that area as long as order was maintained. On July 3 he issued a circular note to the other powers offering cooperation with allied military forces in rescuing the Peking foreign community, but stressing that the United States was willing to work with all local Chinese officials "not in overt collusion with rebellion" to restore peace to China and preserve its territorial integrity. The circular, which in effect attempted to link American actions with the recent Open Door Notes, did not require a response and for the most part did not receive any.

On July 20 Chinese ambassador Wu T'ing-fang handed Secretary Hay a letter addressed to the president from the emperor of China asking for assistance in ending the crisis. The message had an almost pathetic tone:

We have just received a telegraphic memorial from our envoy, Wu Ting-fang, and it is highly gratifying to us to learn that the United States Government, having in view the friendly relations between the two countries, has taken a deep interest in the present situation. Now China, driven by the irresistible course of events, has unfortunately incurred well-nigh universal indignation. For settling the present difficulty China places special reliance in the United States. We address this message to your excellency in all sincerity and candidness, with the hope that your excellency will devise measures and take the initiative in bringing about a concert of the powers for the restoration of order and peace.[2]

This letter, along with similar notes to several of the other powers, had been sent in response to the viceroys' appeals that the court initiate steps toward negotiations. On July 23 Washington replied, agreeing to cooperate

under the same conditions Hay had insisted on to Li
Hung-chang: that the allied governments be assured that
their diplomatic representatives were alive and well, that
they be allowed free communication with them, and that
the Chinese government cooperate with the allied forces
in their mission to Peking.

The tragedy ultimately proved to be too many
players—all with different motives—involved in the game.
Li Hung-chang could hardly speak for the court, for the
latter was still badly divided over peace and war. The refusal of the ministers to leave Peking was based on their
quite realistic fear that the militants in the Forbidden City
would seize upon the opportunity to carry out a mass
massacre. On the other hand, John Hay could not speak
for Washington's allies, many of whom wished to impose
harsher conditions on China. Indeed, in responding to the
imperial request for assistance in ending the crisis, the
French government had demanded as conditions for
opening negotiations not only a guarantee of security for
the diplomatic personnel but also a total cessation of hostilities, removal from office of the militants under Prince
Tuan, and a repression of all Boxer activities. Unless all
these conditions were met, the French warned, the allies
would continue their advance to Peking.

The continuous rivalry between the powers seemed
almost as much of an impediment to peace as did the
impasse between the allies and the Manchu dynasty. The
British, who had sympathized with the reformists in 1898
and protested against the *de facto* deposition of the emperor at that time, distrusted Tz'u Hsi, blamed her for the
war, and were inclined to press for her removal from
power. Foreign Secretary Salisbury was for this reason
reluctant to undertake negotiations with the court
before a significant military victory had been achieved.
The French, on the other hand, suspected the British of
having used K'ang Yu-wei's reform party to insinuate
themselves at court, and they were suspicious of British
motives in demanding the removal of Tz'u Hsi from power.

Paris was inclined to see the empress dowager's 1898 coup as a move not against the reformers but against British interference at court. Tz'u Hsi was viewed as an unwilling participant in the Boxer conflict. "This superior woman," said one eminent French diplomat, "has always been favorable to the foreigners. She is the first victim of the insurrection."[3] Thus, whereas the British were inclined to resist negotiations with the Chinese government and to press for the restoration of the emperor to the throne, there was some sentiment in France in support of the empress dowager to avoid the future British domination of the Chinese empire.

Other powers ranged themselves on the different sides in line with their own interests and prejudices. The Russians provisionally supported the French, not only because the two had been cooperating in the European balance of power, but also because they did not want to lose the "special relationship" they felt they had in Peking since the negotiations that ended the Lorcha Arrow War in 1860. For that reason, the Russians were inclined to equivocate over final solutions until they saw what developed, and to imply to the court that they alone were sympathetic to Chinese interests. The Germans and the Japanese—in part because of the murder of their envoys in Peking—took a harsher view and were inclined to press the conflict to a military conclusion. Berlin, in particular, seemed to take a callous joy in exacting retribution. Emperor William II made history when he gave a send-off speech to German troops leaving for Asia:

Even as, a thousand years ago, the Huns under their King Attila made such a name for themselves as still resounds in terror through legend and fable, so may the name of Germany resound through Chinese history a thousand years from now so that never again will a Chinese dare to so much as look askance at a German.

In the kaiser's opinion, negotiations were useless. The only solution was to storm and then raze the Chinese capital. While the diplomats and the viceroys sparred, the allied commanders in Tientsin gradually began to look to the task before them. There was a curious sense of lassitude among the allied forces in north China after the occupation of Tientsin. On hearing the rumor that the foreign community in Peking had been massacred, many felt that the situation had lost its urgency. Even after learning that the report was false, the general feeling was that the chances of rescuing the legations were remote.

Along with such feelings of anticlimax, there were concrete disagreements over the timing of the planned advance to the capital.[4] The main issue was simple: how many troops would be required for the final assault on Peking? By the end of July there were approximately seventeen thousand foreign troops in north China, with reinforcements arriving daily. The largest force was Japanese, with eight thousand men. Also present were four thousand Russians, two thousand British, seventeen hundred Americans, and smaller contingents of French, Germans, Austrians, and Italians.

For some, the number of troops deployed was sufficient to justify an immediate advance. General A. F. Gaselee, commander of British forces, wanted to move immediately, as did the highest ranking American officer at Tientsin, Colonel A. S. Daggett, commander of the newly arrived 14th Infantry regiment. Daggett's views were not necessarily decisive, however. He would soon be succeeded in command by General Adna Chaffee, sent by Washington to head U.S. forces for the advance to Peking. Others, notably the Russian and Japanese military leaders, were more reluctant to move without bolstering allied strength. General Linievitch, the Russian commander, felt that a minimum of eighty thousand troops was needed before an advance could be made; it would have been impossible to assemble such a force before early September. The Japanese commander, Lieutenant General Yamaguchi, tended to agree, suggesting August 15 as a departure date, but he did not appear to feel strongly about it.

Obviously a compromise was in order. In the back of

everyone's mind was the expected beginning of the rainy season, due in early August. The rains would raise the level of the Pei Ho, thus minimizing the problem of maintaining supplies, but they would also make the ground treacherous and advance on foot much more difficult. At a meeting on July 27 the allied commanders reached a compromise. They agreed to prepare for an advance, but the date of actual departure was left undecided. In the meantime, reinforcements would be arriving, tending to reassure those with doubts.

Assembling more allied forces in China was not an easy job. The British, involved in a war with the Boers in South Africa, had only Indian troops available. The Americans, still engaged in pacifying the rebel movement under Emilio Aguinaldo in the Philippines, were hesitant to add significantly to their own contingent. Earlier, military commanders in China had recommended that the United States provide ten thousand out of a total force of eighty thousand. John Hay had vetoed the suggestion on the grounds that it would put American participation at a higher level than all the other powers except Russia and Japan. He did reluctantly agree to send two more infantry regiments, a battery of artillery, and more provisions. (The total U.S. force in China was thus composed of the 9th Infantry and the 1st Marines already in Tientsin; two battalions of the 14th Infantry and Battery F of the 15th Artillery from the Philippines; and another marine battalion and the 6th cavalry regiment sent directly from the United States.) The French, too, limited their participation, sending only infantry units from Indochina. The Germans had mobilized several thousand troops with considerable fanfare, but few actually arrived, and Italy and Austria announced that they had no troops available.

The Russians and the Japanese were in the best position to strengthen the allied force. The Russians, however, were limited by distance, so only the Japanese actually had virtually unlimited resources. They were also completely

willing to participate, so it was eventually to Japan that
the powers turned. On July 22 the British appealed to
Tokyo to provide more troops. Tokyo agreed on the condition that the allies would finance the deployment of
the troops and that there were no objections from the
other powers. The latter condition referred particularly to
the Russians and the French, who were notoriously sensi-
tive about the presence of their many rivals in Asia. The
reaction of the other powers to a large increase in the
Japanese role was not totally enthusiastic. Neither the
Russians nor the French were happy about it. They
believed that the Japanese were being used as a stalking
horse for British designs in north China, but they were
apparently embarrassed to seem too suspicious and gave
their reluctant approval. London thereupon informed the
Japanese that there were no objections and promised that
outside financial assistance would be secured. With all
possible obstacles removed, the Japanese prepared to increase the size of their troop strength at Tientsin to
twenty thousand. The next question was whether they
would arrive in time to permit an allied offensive before
the flood season made the north China plain virtually im-
passable.

On July 29 General Adna Chaffee arrived from the
United States to command the American forces in China.
Chaffee was a cavalry officer who had seen service in the
Civil War and the Spanish-American conflict. He posed
no objections to an early advance by the allies, although
he did request more artillery from American naval units
in the harbor at Taku.[5] On the day of Chaffee's arrival the
allied commanders held a conference and abandoned as
premature a possible departure date of August 1. They
agreed to meet daily and to make their final decision on
the basis of majority rule.

When they met again on August 1, General Linievitch,
the Russian commander, wanted to delay further in order to
assemble more troops. But by this time General Yamaguchi

General Adna Chaffee, chief of
American military forces in the
advance to Peking (*Leslie's
Weekly,* August 4, 1900, p. 86)

Colonel Emerson Liscum,
killed during the assault on
Tientsin (*Leslie's Weekly,*
August 4, 1900, p. 10)

had changed his mind and was anxious to get started. He
announced that he would order his troops to advance on
August 4, whether or not the remainder of the allies joined
him. He was supported by Gaselee and Chaffee, both of
whom were worried about the foreign community in Peking;
a communication from the legations reported that the
situation was critical. Outnumbered, the Russians agreed
to a joint departure on August 4.

The allies held a predeparture meeting on the third
and made final preparations. By now the allied force stood
at slightly over twenty thousand men. Japanese strength
had reached ten thousand, the Russians were at five
thousand, the British three thousand, the Americans about
twenty-five hundred, and French Indochina had sent eight
hundred Vietnamese. The nomimal commander of the entire expeditionary force was to be British General Gaselee,
but it was agreed that majority rule, reached at a conference

of commanders each evening, would determine all major decisions. They would follow the same route chosen by a previous generation of allied forces in 1860—up the Pei Ho from Tientsin to Peking. The choice of the river route (as opposed to the railroad) would permit use of sampans and junks to facilitate the supplying of the troops. The rainy season was about to start.

August 4, the day on which the offensive was to be opened, dawned hot and humid. By midday the temperature would reach 104 degrees. The allied troops drew up for the advance along the following lines: The first day's march would follow the path of the river, almost due north from Tientsin. The left wing, following the west bank of the river, would be represented by the Americans, the British, and the Japanese. The Russians and the French, along with a token contingent of Austrians and Italians, would form the right wing and advance along the east bank. The Germans were not represented.

Gaselee's plan was fairly simple. He intended to set a fast pace, stopping only when his forces encountered resistance. Once the initial assault had broken through the enemy's lines, he would resume the rapid advance, calling on the rear echelons to mop up. In advance of the main column, the cavalry units—a regiment of Japanese, a few Cossacks, and the Bengal Lancers—would fan out in reconnaissance until the enemy had been located.

The allied units moved out at 3:00 P.M., maintaining a steady pace along both sides of the river. They passed through a seemingly endless series of small villages, situated alongside fields of grain nearly ten feet high. A brief rainshower late in the afternoon cooled the air, but it also made the roads slippery, hindering cart traffic. Fortunately, most of the supplies were being towed upriver by Chinese coolies. During this first day the allies met no resistance from the Chinese, whose own line of defense stretched from northeast to southwest across the railway, with their right flank resting on the river embankment, their left astride the railway. Most of the Chinese forces were concentrated in the center at the point where the railroad crossed the river just south of Yangts'un. At that point they had constructed an elaborate series of trenches and earthworks.

The first night they camped about four miles out of Tientsin, near the Hsi-ku arsenal, which had been held by the Russians since July 26. For most of the force the day had been uneventful, with only the Japanese troops engaging in a brief skirmish with Chinese about two miles to the north of the arsenal. The allied forces moved out at two o'clock the next morning, during a thunderstorm. (Early departures would be the rule during the entire campaign. The troops could thus complete the bulk of each day's march before the heat shimmering on the north China plain became unbearable.) The Japanese column advanced on the right bank and immediately encountered Chinese troops at the town of Nansung, but the latter fled without offering resistance. Before daybreak they encountered Chinese defenses at Peitsang. The allies had expected resistance here, and the entire force on the left bank attacked the Chinese positions with artillery fire and bayonet charges. By midday they had broken through and occupied the town of Peitsang. The Japanese had borne the brunt of the fighting and suffered fairly heavy casualties—60 dead and an estimated 240 wounded. British and American losses were minimal. On the opposite bank forces under French and Russian command were hindered by the difficult ground and did not contact the Chinese, who had retreated before the advancing allies. That night the allied forces bivouacked at Peitsang. Their objective for the following day was the rail and river junction of Yangts'un.

At a meeting of the allied commanders that night it was agreed that the Japanese would continue their advance along the west bank, while the British and Americans would cross over to the east bank to join the Russians and the French in the expected battle before Yangts'un. Their precise objective would be to seize the railroad bridge where the Tientsin-Peking rail line crossed over to the west bank of the Pei Ho. Advancing along the rail line, the right flank of the allied force came within striking distance of the Chinese defense lines just before noon. This time the British and the Americans were called upon to lead the attack, with support from the Russians and the French. In the assault the latter took the left flank, while the Anglo-American force attacked on the center and the right. Advancing in extended order, rather than in the close order utilized by the Japanese on the previous day (in the belief that the concentration of forces had resulted in the heavy Japanese casualties), the allies were able to make steady progress through the Chinese lines. They achieved their objective well before sundown. Losses were fairly light — the Americans suffered 72 casualties, the British 45, and the Russians 118. According to contemporary accounts, the advancing units were troubled as much by heat exhaustion as by enemy bullets. Also, the first major problems caused by a lack of coordination between the various national units occurred in the attack. During the American advance on the right flank, an artillery barrage by the British and Russians landed among the Americans, killing four and wounding several more. It took some time to inform the gunners of their mistake and order them to stop. The blunder occurred when a Russian battery asked a nearby battery of the British Royal Artillery for the range. Receiving the distance in yards, they mistook it for meters, and their shells therefore fell short and landed among the rapidly advancing Americans.[6]

The defeat of Yangts'un was a bitter one for Yü Lu, governor-general of Chihli Province. He had hoped to make a stand there and arrest the advance of the allied forces. The collapse of the Chinese resistance brought him to despair, and that evening he committed suicide — in a coffin shop.

The allies had agreed to remain at Yangts'un for a full day in order to call up reinforcements and supplies and to provide the exhausted troops with their first day of rest since the beginning of the march. The Chinese resistance had been lighter than expected, particularly at Yangts'un where they had drawn up their forward defense line. But the problem of heat prostration had been unexpectedly serious, General Gaselee decided that a full day at camp was justified for re-forming the allied lines and bringing up the supply train, which had already fallen to the rear.

Taking advantage of the day of inactivity, August 7, the generals held a conference. They agreed to continue the advance to the commercial city of Tungchow further up the river and to regroup and hold another conference there. There was some grumbling at the rapid pace of the advance. General Frey complained that his Vietnamese troops were unable to keep up and would be compelled to spend an extra day at Yangts'un before following the allied forces. For the most part, however, there was a feeling of impatience in the allied camp, with almost everyone anxious to reach Peking and the final objective.

As the new advance began the Japanese once again took the lead, followed by the Russians, the British, and the Americans. As usual, the allied column got underway before daybreak and, for the last time, crossed over to the west bank of the river. The pattern was now familiar. The forces passed through fields of corn ten to fifteen feet high and tiny villages with houses built of mud, wood, or brick. What one observer called "the dust of ages" rose at every step. It was tempting to advance along the raised roadway, which, at six to twelve feet above the surrounding country-side, was cooler and less dusty than a march through the surrounding fields. But the road was crooked (to confuse the spirits, according to rumor) and took longer, so the dusty cornfields must be endured. The heat was still a serious problem, particularly to the Russians. They were forced to make frequent halts, keeping the pace down to a mile an hour. The slowness of the Russian advance caused some grumbling among the British and Americans to the rear, for it forced them to do their own marching during the hottest hours of the day. Drinking water, too, was a problem. For the most part, the troops got their drinking water (and did their bathing) in the Pei Ho, which was full of the bloated corpses of Chinese floating down to the sea. Even boiled water was covered with a thick layer of scum.

In the vanguard, the Japanese were less bothered by weather conditions. General Yamaguchi, determined to keep up the pressure on the Chinese to prevent them from regrouping to make a firm stand, urged his troops to keep up a rapid pace, while continuing to harass the retreating enemy forces. Conspicuous on this day were the superior conditioning and organization of the Japanese (according to contemporary observers, the Japanese wore backpacks considerably lighter, yet just as efficient as those worn in other allied units). At times the leading Japanese mounted units were more than three miles in front of the main body of allied infantry. Once contact with the enemy was established, the infantry units rushed to the front line, fanned out, and advanced on a broad front, cleaning out the scattered resistance as they progressed. The total advance for August 8 was twelve miles.

On the ninth the allies pushed on to the town of Hohsiwu, about a day's march south of Tungchow. There Li Ping-heng, just arrived at the battlefront to take command of Chinese forces, hoped to slow down the allied advance. The allies began with a heavy artillery bombardment on Hohsiwu and followed with a furious cavalry charge by the Japanese units and the Bengal Lancers. This charge turned the flank of the defenders (the allies had now discovered that flank attacks were the most effective tactics against the relatively immobile Chinese forces) and dispersed the Chinese troops, who retreated in disorder.

On the following morning, August 10, the allied column advanced to Ma T'ou, over halfway between Yangts'un and Tungchow and the last major obstacle before the walls of the capital. Here Li Ping-heng hoped to halt the allied advance. To impede the allies' progress and prevent them from entering Ma T'ou, he cut ditches and diverted water from the canals just south of the city. The weather had been dry, however, so this ploy had little effect.

As the allies neared the city they began to encounter stragglers, an indication that the Chinese army was in the process of disintegrating. This was a promising sign that there would be no further resistance on the road to Peking. According to a report by General Li Ping-heng, the retreating Chinese soldiers did nothing but plunder and burn the towns as they passed through. Li was in despair, claiming that he lacked sufficient authority to take decisive action, that he lacked competent commanders, and that his troops were totally unmanageable. It would be hard to assemble the scattered forces of the empire, he said, but he would do his best though it was, perhaps, already too late.

On August 11 the allies took another giant step toward their ultimate objective and reached Chiangchiawan, just south of Tungchow. Rain had brought cooler temperatures, providing badly needed relief for the troops. Here Li Ping-heng had decided to make a last desperate attempt to halt the inexorable advance of the allies toward the capital, but he had not reckoned with the mood of his troops. Law and order had disintegrated, and the Chinese soldiers were interested only in booty — or in flight. When the Japanese, leading the allied advance, arrived at the gates of Tungchow, they found that the Chinese garrison had already fled but not before despoiling the city and leaving it open to the rampaging Boxers who killed all those suspected of sympathy for the foreigner. The allies marched into Tungchow and completed the rape of the city. General Li Ping-heng, his last hopes for victory smashed, commited suicide.

George Lynch's description of the plundering of Tungchow does not make pleasant reading, but it is too graphic to be passed over:

Going along the streets, we passed groups of soldiers here and there helping themselves to fodder for their horses from the grain shops, breaking open the doors or windows of shops that were closed and ransacking their contents. Hovering around them, vulture-like, were some of the lowest class of the native population, whose desire to share in the spoil was sufficiently strong to overcome their fears . . . .

The human casualties were worse:

Passing along the sunken road between the city wall and some high ground on which houses were built, I could hear the shouts of Russians mingled with screams proceeding from the houses. There was a sheer drop of considerable height between the walls of the houses and the stony road below. At the base of the cliff two Chinese girls were lying. Their legs were bundled under them in a way that showed they had jumped from the height above. From their richly embroidered silken tunics and trousers, their elaborate coiffure and their compressed feet, they were evidently ladies. They were moaning piteously, and one of them appeared to be on the point of death. Their legs or hips had apparently been broken or dislocated by their jump . . . . The hoarse cries of the soldiers, mingled occasionally with a sobbing scream, came from the houses above, telling what they had tried so desperately to escape from.[7]

As the allied advance neared the capital, depression gripped the court. Grand Secretary Jung Lu, who still somehow retained the confidence of the empress dowager, commiserated with her in her anxiety, while at the same time delicately raising the question of what action to take in case of defeat. At first she refused to admit that all was lost and brought up the example of the Han dynasty scholar Chia I, who had used "the five enticements" and "the three manifestations" (seducing the enemy with riches and honeyed words to re-establish friendly relations and causing them to forget their hostility). On hearing the news of Li Ping-heng's defeat before Tungchow, however, she lost heart and considered flight (euphemistically entitled "a journey of inspection" to the provinces) or even suicide (taking the emperor with her). Jung Lu strongly opposed both proposals and appealed to her to take strong action against the militants in order to convince the allies of her good intentions. Tz'u Hsi was unwilling to abandon the militants, however, even though the Boxers were now "wearing thinner than cotton." To the end she seemed incapable of breaking with the antiforeign elements.

As the end neared, the court continued its attempts to reach a settlement on the diplomatic front. It sent out last-minute feelers—through a telegram to foreign capitals and a message to the legations—requesting a cease-fire, and gave Li Hung-chang plenipotentiary powers to negotiate with the foreigners. In reply to the telegram, President McKinley stated that he was willing to mediate if the other powers did not object. In the legation quarter Sir Claude MacDonald agreed to talk with Chinese officials about a cease-fire and suggested a meeting at the British legation on the morning of August 13. But the Chinese members of the Tsungli Yamen, pleading "important official engagements," refused to come. Some observers believed that the Chinese feared being held in the foreign settlement after the close of the meeting.

Elsewhere in China the viceroys had good reasons for actively pursuing a settlement. The situation in central and south China was precarious. The rising sense of danger in early August had led the British to call up three thousand troops from the crown colony of Hong Kong to Shanghai. The local Chinese authorities protested, claiming that they were capable of maintaining law and order themselves, but the British declared that they would take whatever actions were necessary to protect their citizens. Some of the great powers were troubled by the British action. The French, in particular, feared that London was using the crisis as a means of solidifying its control in the Yangtse Valley and dispatched 350 of their own troops to the area as a countermeasure.

Li Hung-chang was the most active of the viceroys on the diplomatic front. He had been ordered to leave Canton to accept his new post as viceroy of Chihli, but he delayed his departure because of the uncertainty at court and his conviction that he could do nothing while the militants

were in control. Convinced that only a military defeat near
the capital would create the necessary conditions for a
settlement, he limited his efforts to studying the attitudes
of the great powers. At the end of July, while in Shanghai
awaiting developments in the north, he became convinced
that the time had come for action and drafted a memorial
to the throne calling for measures which would substan-
tially satisfy most of the conditions posed by the powers
for a settlement of the conflict. He suggested that the
court appoint high officials to escort the foreigners from
the legation quarter to Tientsin, and that it issue a decree
ordering officials in the provinces to protect all foreigners
and suppress the Boxers. In taking this action, Li was
taking quite a risk. His fellow viceroy, Chang Chih-tung,
felt that conciliatory offers from the court were premature
so long as its hands were tied by the Boxers. Li would not
brook delay: "In time of emergency," he said, "there is
no time for hesitation."

As the allied troops neared Peking Li moved on all
fronts. He ordered Chinese diplomatic representatives
abroad to indicate the Chinese government's interest in a
truce. Tokyo and Washington responded to these over-
tures, both suggesting that the Chinese send representatives
to the front to negotiate a cease-fire and the release of the
foreigners in the legation quarter. Li immediately memorialized the throne, advising that officials from the Tsungli
Yamen along with the Commissioner of Customs Sir
Robert Hart (one of the besieged in the legation quarter)
should be sent to negotiate. Hart, for many years an em-
ployee of the Chinese government, was one of the few
foreigners trusted by the court. All of this came too late,
however. While Li's memorial was on its way to Peking,
the allies attacked the city.

After the uneventful occupation of Tungchow on
August 12 the allies held a conference of generals to deter-
mine their next move. Some wanted to continue on to
Peking the following day, but the Russian commander,
General Linievitch, protested (for reasons that would soon

be clear) that his troops needed a day of rest before the final assault. A compromise was reached. August 13 would be devoted to reconnaissance operations ascertaining the nature of the Chinese resistance in the capital area. A decision on whether to advance would be made at a final meeting that evening.

Reconnaissance units sent out toward Peking soon discovered that there would be little resistance from Chinese forces between Tungchow and the capital. But the problem facing the allies was less Chinese resistance than the rivalries among the great powers themselves. Despite the long delays encountered by the allies in their march to Peking, there was intense competition in the race to reach the legation quarter. The Russians and the Japanese, in particular, were determined to carry off the prize, while many of the others, including the Americans, seemed too exhausted to care. To reduce antagonism between the various nationalities, the commanders agreed, at General Gaselee's suggestion, that all the military units would line up at an advance position not far from Peking and then literally wage a footrace to the wall. According to the plan, the Russians were scheduled to advance on a paved road running along the north bank of the Tungchow-Peking Canal. The Japanese would take up a position to their left, but still north of the canal. The British and the Americans were to operate on the south side of the canal, the Americans on a road which ran parallel to the canal and the British to their left on another road about a mile and a half further south. The other nationalities, including the exhausted French troops, would bring up the rear.

As the allied troops awoke at daybreak on the fourteenth to prepare for the final assault on Peking, it soon became evident that the plan formulated the day before had already gone awry. The position that was supposed to be occupied by the Russians on the north bank of the canal was vacant. In their desire to be first over the wall and into the legation quarter, the Russians had jumped the

Fields of corn were interspersed with flooded pools and irrigation ditches. Not until dawn did the Russian forward units, commanded by chief of staff General Vassilevski, manage to come within striking distance of the Peking city wall. At this point the Russians were supposed to head northwest toward the T'ung Chih gate at the northeastern corner of the Tartar city. Instead, they cut to the left toward the American objective, the Tung Pien gate near the juncture of the Tartar city and the native city along the east wall. Here General Vassilevski attempted a frontal attack on the city's defenses. His troops were able to cross the bridge on the moat running along the outer wall and blast through the outer gate. But, like the Japanese at Tientsin, on penetrating the gate they found themselves pinned down in an inner courtyard and exposed to fire from Chinese troops along the city wall above. As day broke they had seized a small portion of the wall near the gate but were unable to advance through the inner gate into the city. They were forced to wait for the arrival of the remaining Russian units under General Linievitch.

The remaining units of the allied force began the advance on schedule. They heard firing to the west but did not realize what had taken place. General Chaffee, commanding the American forces, was unaware that the Russians had attacked the American objective on the wall and saw no need to change his plans because the Russians had left early. Just before daybreak he sent elements of his 6th Cavalry under Captain de Rosey Cabell on reconnaissance toward the city. Two hours later a cavalryman returned to camp and reported that his unit had encountered heavy Chinese resistance and was engaged about two miles east of the city. Cabell and most of his unit, reconnoitering on foot, had been fired upon from a small village and were temporarily pinned down there. Cabell sent back his interpreter to report the situation to General Chaffee, who immediately ordered a battalion of the 14th Infantry under Captain Eastman to rescue "his boys." On their arrival at the village Eastman's men found that Cabell's unit was in no immediate danger but was engaged in a rather desultory exchange of fire with scattered groups of Chinese soldiers on the village rooftops.

By midmorning the American units had reached their assigned position across from the Tung Pien gate. It was then they saw that the Russians were already engaged there and appeared to be "in great confusion," still caught in the *cul de sac* of the inner courtyard of the massive gate. Moreover, there were no British forces on the Americans' left flank. Gaselee had decided to let his units fend for themselves. In consequence, they had been slow to leave camp and had not yet arrived before the city wall.

Left to his own devices, Colonel Daggett of the 14th Infantry decided to move the American objective slightly to the south and launch an attack at a point on the wall midway between the Tung Pien gate and the gate further to the south—the Sha Wo Men. By this plan, the Americans would enter the native city, rather than the Tartar city to the north. Leading the advance was E Company of the 14th Infantry. Despite heavy fire from the wall they managed to cross the moat and reach the base of the wall without serious casualties. There Daggett faced a problem. The thirty-foot wall appeared to be fairly smooth, and he had no scaling ladders or grappling hooks. The problem was resolved by the company bugler, Calvin Titus, who volunteered to climb the wall and see if there were any Chinese troops at the top. Finding footholds in the crumbling mortar between the bricks, Titus managed to make it to the top without incident. He found the top of the wall clear of troops and called down, "The coast is clear, come on up." Other men from the company began to scale the wall, and by 11:00 A.M. fire from Daggett's men began forcing the Chinese troops to retreat from the wall atop the Tung Pien gate further north, thus allowing the Russians below to enter the city.

To the south the American 9th Infantry and units of marines had reached the wall, with the British now in sight to the left at the Sha Wo gate. When American com-

mand headquarters arrived, a section of the 6th Artillery
began to fight its way into the southeast sector of the
Chinese city. By midafternoon U.S. artillery units were
beginning to shell the Ha Ta gate, on the Tartar city wall
just southeast of the legation quarter. As the American
activities preoccupied Chinese forces in the area of the east
wall, the Russians finally managed to break through at
the Tung Pien gate. Inside the city, however, they were
once again pinned down in the narrow streets.

On the far right of the allied front the Japanese were
meeting some of the heaviest resistance of the day. Approaching the Chi Hua gate at the center of the wall
forming the eastern boundary of the Tartar city, they ran
into heavy fire and were forced to wait for the arrival of
their artillery units. After extensive shelling, Japanese
engineers were able to blow up the gate, and at nightfall,
Japanese infantry units finally penetrated into the city.

After breaking into the Chinese city American
units of the 14th Infantry and a battery of artillery under
Captain Henry Reilly found themselves milling around in
the complex alleys of the Chinese city. Just below the
south wall of the Tartar city they were able to clear Chinese
forces out of the area and, firing from doorways and rooftops, gradually work their way westward. Except for the
section adjacent to the legation quarter to the west, the
wall was still in Chinese hands. By midafternoon the
American artillery units began to bombard Chinese positions on the wall, soon destroying the pagoda tower above
the Ha Ta gate.

Ironically, it was the British, who had still not arrived when the Americans began to scale the outer wall,
who were the first into the legation quarter. After starting
late from camp and then briefly losing their way, at about
noon they reached the Sha Wo gate on the east wall of
the Chinese city south of the Americans. To their good
fortune, there were no Chinese troops at the gate (apparently the Chinese were concentrated at the main
eastern entrances to the Tartar city), and the British were

Men of Captain Reilly's artillery battery scaling the wall into the
Imperial City (*Leslie's Weekly*, October 27, 1900, p.296)

able to open the gate and enter the city unopposed. As they approached the Tartar wall they saw a sailor on the wall waving a signal flag and gesturing toward a water gate at the base of the wall below. This was the sluice gate for the Imperial Canal which ran directly south from the Forbidden City and through the center of the legation quarter. (The good fortune of the British troops was not entirely an accident. British minister MacDonald had sent a dispatch to Gaselee informing him that the water gate was the easiest entry into the legation area.)

The British troops, mostly Indian sepoys, worked their way down into the ditch below the wall. There they encountered American marines inside the gate trying to cut through the heavy iron grating that barred passage through the tunnel. The marines managed to force out a narrow opening, and the invading British troops passed through and emerged into the legation quarter where they were mobbed by an ecstatic crowd of defenders. After six weeks of siege the legations had finally been relieved.

For the foreigners in the legations, the rescue had come none too soon. After Li Ping-heng had arrived at court, hostility in the capital toward the besieged community intensified. Curious intervals of quiet were punctuated by fierce attacks, particularly on August 10 and again on the night of the thirteenth when shelling on the legations made it impossible for the defenders to sleep. Conciliatory messages had continued to arrive from the Tsungli Yamen, adding tantalizing hope to the foreigners' growing anxiety. The besieged community also received messages from the allied forces beyond the wall and were aware of their impending arrival. But only when they first heard distant firing early on the morning of August 14 did they realize that rescue was at hand. Seventy-four residents of the foreign community had died in the siege. Of these, eight—including several infants—had died of disease.

For the remainder of the day the allies made few attempts to wipe out opposition elsewhere in the city. The

Americans arrived in the legation quarter soon after the British, to their great disappointment. The Russians and the Japanese gradually worked their way toward the legations, burning and sacking the eastern quarters of the Tartar city. From the legations, looting parties were sent out to punish the Chinese for their temerity in opposing the powers. Lancelot Giles, a young British consular officer, described the days following the arrival of the allies:

That afternoon I went with the party who cleared the wall, to the Ch'ien Men. Some Chinese soldiers ran out in the yard below the gate and started firing up at us. They were all shot.

Two Maxims [a type of machine gun invented by the American explosives expert, Hudson Maxim] were fixed up on Ch'ien Men and turned on a stream of people who were hurrying across the inner Palace yard. About fifty to seventy rifles were turned on them too. Any amount slaughtered.

Every day looting parties go out and get what they can. I have done some splendid looting already. You wait and trust to me, before you speak.[8]

By their actions, it was hard to distinguish the Boxers from the foreigners.

In the battle to reach the legations the British had been the first to enter the quarter and effect the rescue, but it was undoubtedly the Japanese, more than any others, who enhanced their reputation during the conflict with their skill and tenacity in combat and their graciousness toward the conquered enemy.

On the morning of August 15 General Chaffee, under the orders of Minister Conger, set himself to clearing Chinese troops from the imperial city, directly to the north of the legation quarter. Cannon were placed on the south wall at the Ch'ien Men to shell the last redoubt of the defenders. Meanwhile, units of the 14th Infantry, supported by a battery of Captain Reilly's artillery, began to beat their way northward to the entrance of the Forbidden City. At the first gate they destroyed a wooden door several inches thick and covered with sheet iron. The Americans surged inside, only to find themselves in a

Ch'i Hua gate on the east wall of the Tartar city through which the Japanese troops entered Peking (*Leslie's Weekly*, September 1, 1900, cover)

courtyard. This was to be the pattern for the next hour, as the troops encountered gate after gate, each leading into an inner courtyard closer to the imperial palace. Throughout the assault they were met with intense fire from Chinese units in the vicinity which killed several Americans, including Captain Reilly himself. They had approached the final barrier to the palace when they received word that the allied commanders had agreed to call off the attack. With no little grumbling—the Americans may well have harbored dreams of rich booty—they retired to the legation quarter for the night.

There may have been several reasons for the decision to arrest the American advance. In the first place, the French and the Russians wanted to take a conciliatory attitude toward the court. Any overt invasion of the sacred inner sanctum of the Forbidden City would have further alienated the empress dowager and perhaps made a reasonable settlement with her impossible. But more mundane factors may have influenced the decision—notably the other powers' fear that the Americans would steal off with all the loot. Few observers questioned the fact that Chaffee's primary motive was glory, particularly since he had earlier refused a French request to participate in the action.

Not until the second day of the occupation of Peking did the allies remember the three thousand Christians, protected by a handful of Italian and French marines, who had been besieged in the Peitang Cathedral two miles to the northwest of the legations. Since the beginning of the siege they had been isolated from the legation quarter, and the attacks and the deprivation there had been even more intense than in the quarter itself. For several weeks the defenders were holed up within the stout walls of the cathedral; they were almost constantly under attack. By one estimate, over twenty-four hundred shells had fallen on the building during the siege. Among the defenders, several hundred Chinese were killed or had died of starvation, while eleven foreign soldiers were killed and twelve wounded. One of the casualties was French marine captain Paul Henry, who had bravely kept up the spirits of the defenders until he was killed by a rifle bullet on July 30. Most tragic, perhaps, were the deaths of over 150 Chinese children, many as the result of a mine explosion under the church. By the end, the survivors in the cathedral had almost reached the limit of their food rations and were reduced to eating grass and flower-root soup. To their everlasting credit, the besieged community had shared their rations on an equal basis—a lesson in brotherhood for their counterparts in the legation quarter who were, at least relatively speaking, more fortunate.

The rescue mission to relieve the cathedral was sent from the legations on the morning of August 15. Over twelve hundred troops, mostly French and Japanese, converged on the church and found it still under fire from Boxers. A few bursts from the rapid-fire guns of the foreigners scattered the attackers and the siege was relieved. At first the defenders seemed unable to believe that they had been rescued. The first foreign troops to approach the cathedral had been Japanese, and because of their Oriental features the residents thought they were Chinese soldiers and refused to let them in.

The relief had come none too soon. Monsignor Favier, who had borne the attacks on his flock with courage and dignity, did, however, express one small poignant regret. "It is almost a pity that we were not all massacred. We should have died martyrs," he said.

Chapter Nine

The Aftermath

O nce the seizure of Peking by the allies had become a near certainty, the empress dowager
began to make plans to flee the capital. Jung Lu
at court and the viceroys in the central provinces had protested this decision, contending that she
would be better off staying in Peking and personally ordering the punishment of those most responsible for
promoting the conflict. But by August 10 Tz'u Hsi had decided to transfer her entourage to Sian, several hundred
miles to the west in Shensi Province. She had selected
several Manchu officials to serve as a caretaker government
during her absence, including Jung Lu, Hsü T'ung, and the
militant K'ang I.

By the afternoon of August 14 further delay seemed
impossible. At 4:00 P.M. two of the empress dowager's
courtiers informed her that American troops were approaching the gate of the imperial palace and beseeched
her to leave the Forbidden City. Shortly afterward the
Americans retired, but the reprieve was obviously temporary. That evening Tz'u Hsi called a meeting of the
Grand Council to inform the members of her decision to
leave. With many of the members in flight (Jung Lu him-

Cartoon of a Boxer at the feet of Uncle Sam, entitled "Justice or Mercy" (*Leslie's Weekly*, September 14, 1900, cover)

self was attempting to rally the troops in a final defense of the capital), only three attended. Before daybreak the next morning the empress dowager, accompanied by the emperor and a small retinue, left in a nondescript cart. They were dressed in Chinese peasant clothes in case they were apprehended by allied troops.

At the last minute the emperor's favorite consort, the Pearl Concubine, protested the decision to abandon Peking. She begged Tz'u Hsi to allow the emperor to remain at the palace to take part in the negotiations. Tz'u Hsi had long hated the Pearl Concubine, for Kuang Hsü had always preferred her company over that of his official wife who had been hand-picked by his dowager aunt. Angered now at the temerity of the younger woman, the empress dowager ordered her thrown down a well on the palace grounds. The emperor was heartbroken, but his will to resist his powerful aunt had long since been broken, and he departed with her without protest.

At 8:00 A.M. the imperial party stopped at the summer palace, in the hills west of Peking. They then continued on to Kalgan in Inner Mongolia, to T'ai Yüan, and then on to Sian, arriving on October 26. The party on the "journey of inspection" had gradually grown into a retinue of a thousand, including several dukes and high officials. The court and administration were set up at Sian for the duration of the crisis.

The empress dowager had turned to Li Hung-chang to find a way out of the morass. On August 19 she had issued a decree ordering him to initiate peace negotiations with the allies: "The minister has been well known for his loyalty and respected by the foreigners. Now that the country has come to such a situation, how he should exert himself." A few days later she had given him full powers to negotiate without interference by the court.

Tz'u Hsi chose Li Hung-chang because she considered him to be the one Chinese most acceptable to the foreigners. In this assumption, however, she was not entirely correct. In many world capitals Li was distrusted and was not a popular choice for chief negotiator for the Chinese government. Some considered him corrupt and a creature of the court, appointed by Prince Tuan to deprive the allies of their justly earned victory. Others, notably the British, believed him to be pro-Russian. (Earlier, he had accepted payment from the Russians in return for a negotiated agreement to build the Manchurian railway.) It would later become clear that Li did not favor the Russians. In fact, he had serious doubts about their good intentions. Because he considered them to be the most dangerous of China's adversaries, he was careful to avoid antagonizing them.

Li Hung-chang was in no hurry to go north to assume charge of the negotiations.[1] He was aware that some of the powers opposed his appointment. Li felt, with some reason, that remaining in Shanghai and refusing to go to Tientsin until all the allies had accepted his credentials as plenipotentiary might bring the latter around to accepting him.

Although Li Hung-chang remained where he was, he made strenuous peace-making efforts on the diplomatic front. When organized Chinese resistance around Peking collapsed, he sent a message to all the powers asking them to cease military operations and begin negotiations, since their main objective of relieving the legations had been realized. With victory assured, however, the allies felt no sense of urgency in sitting down at the conference table. Li was informed that negotiations could not begin until the allied governments had an opportunity to discuss war aims among themselves. The only positive response came from the United States, which indicated that, once China had demonstrated its capacity to maintain law and order, the United States would be willing to begin negotiations on the basis of the American circular message of July 3. The other powers were more cautious. Many were indeed uncertain about accepting Li Hung-chang as plenipotentiary. The general feeling seemed to be that no negotiations could begin until Chinese resistance had been, in the words of Sir Claude MacDonald, "disheartened and completely crushed."

In an effort to win over the recalcitrant foreigners, the empress dowager attempted to persuade Sir Robert Hart to act as an associate plenipotentiary. Hart demurred but did offer to persuade Prince Ch'ing to serve in his place. The prince, however, was in hiding, possibly because he feared the complexity of the duties involved. By early September he had been located and reluctantly agreed to accept the position.

Li waited in vain for the powers to send word that they had accepted his appointment. Finally, in mid-September, he decided to leave Shanghai for Tientsin—ostensibly to take up his post as viceroy of Chihli. He arrived in Tientsin on September 20, but he did not leave for Peking until early October. According to Chester Tan, whose *The Boxer Catastrophe* is one of the standard works on the war, the Germans intended to seize Li during his journey and retain him as a prisoner of war but were dissuaded by their fear of antagonizing the Russians.

Li's delay in traveling north has been criticized by some observers as a hindrance in initiating peace negotiations. But it is clear that the allies themselves were in no hurry to sit down with Chinese representatives to work out a settlement. Some were simply waiting for law and order to be established first. Others wanted to teach the Chinese a lesson they would never forget. Even those who supported Li had their own partisan interests. The Russians, in particular, had designs of their own. They had shown a willingness to cooperate with Li and informed him through the Chinese envoy at St. Petersburg that Russia would pursue a moderate policy designed to assist him in reining in the demands of the other powers. Li had no illusions about Russian intentions, but he lacked confidence about the support he would receive from other capitals in resisting demands from St. Petersburg. His was not an enviable position.

THE PACIFICATION OF PEKING

In Peking the situation was still chaotic. Rampaging bands of Boxers, joined by deserters from regular units, roamed the streets, looting and killing at random. All semblance of authority seemed to have disappeared. The Manchu nobles and high Chinese officials had either fled or committed suicide. Sometimes whole families took their lives. The women were in the most tragic position, for they feared for their lives yet were often unable to flee because of their bound feet.

Under such conditions the first responsibility of the allied occupation forces was to restore law and order. On August 16 Peking was divided into occupation districts— British, French, Japanese, Russian, and American. (The Germans received a zone later, on their arrival.) The looting was not stopped by the partition; it simply became more systematic. Each nation now engaged in the task of despoiling the citizens of its own zone of occupation. By contemporary accounts the Russians and the French were the most flagrant of the booty-hunters. In his massive work on the Chinese Empire, Hosea Ballou Morse quotes a comment in the *Japan Daily Mail* about the "ferocity and callous cruelty dispensed by the Russians." The Germans were apparently not much better. Arriving two thousand strong at the end of August, the German troops appeared to be resentful that they had missed the action (other sources claim they wanted to revenge the assassination of their envoy and to demonstrate the strength and will of Germany). They were so efficient at picking over their own area that countless Chinese citizens allegedly fled into the American zone adjacent to the German district.

The conduct of the Americans and the British was somewhat better—the former used the proceeds of their loot to feed the poor—but it was the Japanese, as had been the case throughout the war, who were the true exceptions. Their behavior in their own district was exemplary.

The military command seized government stores of silk and grain but rigorously prohibited private looting and cruelty to local citizens. The Japanese were the first to bring order to their own district of occupation.

Only one area was spared from the general destruction. The Forbidden City, including the imperial palace itself, was declared off-limits to looting parties. Each nation received a portion of the palace grounds as a part of its occupation district, and the allies, dressed in full regalia, made a token inspection of the premises, but no looting took place.

The other major responsibility of the occupation forces was to bring Chinese resistance to an end. Although the court had fled and most of the Boxer units had disintegrated, melting back into the countryside, scattered resistance to the foreign occupation was still in evidence. In Peking occasional incidents continued through September. The foreign soldiers had difficulty discriminating between the enemy and the harmless citizen, for the resistance elements frequently dressed in civilian clothing. This led to predictable consequences—many innocent Chinese were shot by jittery troops suspicious of all natives and not inclined to give them the benefit of the doubt. Nor were the converts who had been through the siege spared. One was held up three times on the streets by foreign troops who each time relieved him of all he had in his possession.

Outside the capital organized resistance continued in some areas, particularly in the suburbs of Peking. Armed bands of Boxers, often reinforced by army deserters, roamed the countryside around the city, supporting themselves in the time-worn manner by despoiling the local villages of food and property. Some Boxer groups attempted to flee to Shantung, but Governor Yüan Shih-k'ai vigorously drove them out of the territory under his jurisdiction. There seemed to be little centralized direction to these activities. Most of the regular forces had fled west toward Shansi or northwest toward the city of Kalgan. Tung Fu-hsiang, who wanted to hold out, had taken the bulk of his forces to Sian with the court. But the empress dowager apparently had no intention of continuing the struggle, and without her support organized resistance was virtually impossible.

Gradually the allies turned to the problem of pacifying the countryside around Peking and Tientsin. In September three major military operations were undertaken to wipe out the remaining Boxer units in these areas. The first punitive expedition was launched on September 8 at the village of Tu Liu, about fifteen miles southwest of Tientsin. Tu Liu had been one of the major centers of Boxer activity throughout the summer, and in retribution the allied forces burned the village to the ground. Three days later a German force of nearly two thousand men marched to the district of Liang Hsiang, fifteen miles south of the capital on the Peking-Hankow railroad line. Here Chinese forces offered serious resistance, and, after the district town was seized and put to the torch, 170 were tried and executed.

A third major punitive expedition was launched against Boxer headquarters at the village of Pa Ta Chou, in the foothills twelve miles northwest of Peking. The mission was assigned to Major General James Wilson, newly arrived as General Chaffee's second in command. Wilson described the operation in some detail in his memoirs. The expedition consisted of about two thousand men, including two battalions of the 9th Infantry, one of the 14th Infantry, a section of Captain Reilly's artillery battery, and a small detachment of the American 6th Cavalry, along with the Welsh Fusiliers and two battalions of Baluchistanis. Departing at 3:00 P.M. on September 16, Wilson's force set up camp near the Marco Polo bridge. Early the next morning they headed north and reached Pa Ta Chou, where the Boxers were encamped in several temples on a hill overlooking the plains. Wilson divided his forces into two sections. The Baluchistanis and the American 14th Infantry undertook a flanking movement

into the hills to the rear of the temples, while the main
body prepared to make a frontal assault on the temple area
through an opening in the foothills. The operation was a
complete success. The Baluchistanis and the Americans
reached the summit behind the temples and then descended on the position from the rear. Opening fire on the
temples, they cut off the main line of retreat for the
Boxers, who were then assaulted by the main force from
below. The allies suffered no casualties; nine Boxers were
killed.

Investigating the scene, the allied commanders discovered that the temples themselves had served as local
Boxer headquarters, and shrines in the altars at the White
Pagoda—the most famous temple in the vicinity—were
still smoking with incense. Wilson's British adjutant, General
Barrow, asked Wilson permission in the name of Claude
MacDonald to destroy the White Pagoda—a beautiful
structure of white porcelain surrounded by richly carved
marble terraces. In his memoirs Wilson writes that he
could not countenance such action under his command
and asked why it was necessary. Barrow answered that, if
the temple were not destroyed, the Chinese would claim
that their gods were more powerful than ours. Wilson was
not convinced but agreed to withdraw American forces
from the area the next morning, in effect saying that what
the British forces wished to do at that time was their
business. As the Americans prepared for their departure
they saw the pagoda blown up with a charge of gunpowder.

A few other operations took place during the first
month of the occupation, including the seizure of three
forts on the coast which had been inactive during the war.
Throughout the conflict the Chinese defenders had apparently wished to stay out of the fight and had made no
attempt to hinder the allied advance. Now they were taken
with only nominal resistance.

By the end of September most of the allied forces
seemed to have lost heart for further punitive activities in

China. But the arrival of Count Alfred von Waldersee gave new vigor to the pacification process. Von Waldersee, a veteran of the Franco-Prussian War of 1870 and more recently assistant chief of the German General Staff, was appointed commander of all the allied occupation forces in China in early August. There was some slight reluctance on the part of the other powers to grant supreme power in China to the German field marshal, but, since the German minister had been murdered on the streets of Peking, the allies had consistently acceded to German wishes in China whenever possible. It seemed awkward to refuse the appointment after the kaiser had expressly indicated his desire that Waldersee take command. The new German commander arrived in China on September 21 and immediately demonstrated that he intended to punish the Chinese severely for their sins. Throughout October German punitive operations were undertaken in villages and towns in the north China plain. The most severe was directed at the railway hub of Pao Ting Fu, scene of some of the bloodiest massacres of Chinese Christians and Europeans during the Boxer uprising. Count von Waldersee placed himself in charge of this expedition, which left Peking in mid-October. He made an abortive attempt to reach a settlement with the local Chinese authorities. When that failed, his forces devastated the city. Several temples, the city walls, and their towers were all destroyed, and the top administrative officials were condemned to death by a military tribunal set up on the spot. In a final gesture of humiliation, the city's population was compelled to bear the costs of the allied occupation.

Von Waldersee's relentless punishment of the defeated Chinese aroused the distaste of the allied forces in China, and they participated less and less in the German expeditions.[2] Von Waldersee was not to be denied his revenge, however. From mid-December to the following April, forty-six punitive operations were launched against objectives in north China, almost all of them composed entirely of German troops.

THE RUSSIAN CONQUEST OF MANCHURIA

For the Russians, the war did not end with the fall of Peking. To the northeast in Manchuria, it was just beginning. For over a decade Russian influence had been on the rise. By the end of the century the foreign economic interests there were almost entirely Russian, except at the treaty port of Newchwang. These Russian interests were protected by about forty-five hundred railway guards, permitted by the treaty of 1896. In the early summer of 1900 Boxer groups began to congregate and harass foreigners. Mission buildings and foreign commercial establishments were attacked and burned, and several incidents flared between Chinese troops and the Russian railway guards. Concerned, the influential finance minister, Count Witte, strengthened the guard force.

On the seizure of Taku by the allies, the court had ordered Tseng Ch'i, the Manchu commander of Fengtien Province, to arm and organize Boxer units as a supplement to his own forces in the area. By the end of June incidents were becoming more frequent, and Boxers seized several of the railway stations on the spur line running from Harbin to Port Arthur. On August 31 other groups, with the connivance of local officials, attacked a Catholic mission at Mukden and killed five inmates.

In St. Petersburg there was some disagreement over how to handle the situation. Expansion into Manchuria had been a goal for years, but tactics for achieving it were another matter. Witte advocated a peaceful expansion into the area through railroad construction and economic and commercial activities. General Kuropatkin, the war minister, preferred military conquest. The riots in Manchuria played into his hands and compelled the Russian government to make preparations to intervene. On June 11 Witte informed Yang Ju, the Chinese minister in St. Petersburg, that Russia was dispatching troops to the area to suppress the rioters and protect Russian interests. In Canton Li Hung-chang appealed to the Russians to refrain from interfering in the explosive situation, but the latter would agree only to withdraw forces if the local Chinese administration in the area cooperated with them.

In mid-July Russian troops entered Manchuria from several points. One Russian force sailed down the Amur River to Aigun and crossed there into the northern province of Heilungkiang. A short distance upriver, at the Russian city of Blagoveshchensk, Chinese artillery units across the border had been bombarding the city for several days. Panicky Russians turned on the local Chinese population in the city and drove them into the river—allegedly to force them to cross to the Chinese side. In the melee many of the Chinese were shot as they tried to save themselves, some by Chinese troops south of the river who suspected an invasion. Hundreds more were drowned. By some estimates the toll of lives lost was nearly seven thousand. The Chinese attempted to drive back the invading Russians but were themselves forced back, and by late August the Russians had seized the rail center of Tsitsihar, on the Chinese Eastern Railway in Central Manchuria.

A second Russian force crossed the border near the Russian coastal port of Vladivostok into Kirin Province. By late in August they had advanced as far as Ninkuta (now known as Mutanchiang), while a flotilla of Russian ships sailed down the Sungari River from Khabarovsk toward Harbin. On August 2 Harbin was seized, and a few weeks later the city of Kirin fell to the invaders.

Russian forces also moved north from Port Arthur to protect the extensive Russian interests in the Liaotung Peninsula and at Yingkow, the port of Newchwang. Heavy fighting took place in early August, and, after Chinese forces numbering several thousand were driven from the area around Yingkow, the Russians seized administrative control over the city. During the next few weeks Russian troops moved north along the railway, seizing Newchwang, Anshan, and Liaoyang in late September, and entering Mukden on October 2. In less than three months the

Russians had effectively occupied all three provinces of Manchuria.

The Manchu commander of Fengtien Province, Tseng Ch'i, conceded defeat. He had opposed the hostilities in any case and had made vain efforts to suppress the Boxers in the province. In November he agreed to negotiate for peace. On November 30 he reluctantly signed an agreement with Admiral Yevgeni Alexeev providing the Russians with a near protectorate in south Manchuria. The Tseng-Alexeev Convention was not disclosed to the world—or even to the Chinese government.

THE NEGOTIATIONS BEGIN

The occupation forces were settling in for an extended stay, and Li Hung-chang sensed that the time was approaching to begin serious negotiations on a peace agreement. The task would be difficult and complex. Li's main objectives were relatively obvious, if not easy to achieve. He must attempt to protect the dynasty from excessive demands by the allied powers. To do this he would have to convince the court to impose severe penalties on the instigators of the Boxer uprising.

It soon became clear that severe problems would be posed by the court itself, not only because of its isolated location, but because of its composition. Among Tz'u Hsi's principal advisers in Sian were many who had persuaded her to resist the foreign powers throughout the crisis. Prince Tuan was still in evidence, as was the commander of the Kansu army, General Tung Fu-hsiang. The only moderate at court was the aging Chinese grand secretary, Wang Wen-shao. Wang, however, was somewhat weak willed and no match for the militants. Jung Lu was still in Peking with the caretaker government. Official appointments made by the court during the weeks following its arrival in Sian showed that the empress dowager was still dominated by the antiforeign elements in her entourage. According to Hosea Ballou Morse, the court made a deliberate attempt to circumscribe the liberty of action of Liu K'un-yi and Chang Chih-tung, the moderate viceroys in the center, by appointing to their retinue Manchu officials sympathetic to the reactionaries. The court's actions were so transparent that the great powers lodged a protest at one appointment and forced the former to back down.

The growing conflicts among the allies themselves were an additional source of difficulty. The major cause of discord was Russia. The shadow war in Manchuria worried the Japanese, who warned the court against making private arrangements with the Russians and quietly offered to supply weapons to the Chinese in case they were needed. The other powers shared Tokyo's concern about Russian actions, not only in Manchuria, but also south of the Great Wall. There Russian troops appeared to be taking a proprietary attitude toward the Peking-Tientsin railway and the land north of the Pei Ho. At one point, in response to a British complaint, the Russian authorities in north China claimed that they had occupied the land north of Tientsin "by right of conquest" and that this land had therefore become "the property of Russian troops." Such statements obviously risked provoking a dangerous split among the allies as they approached negotiations with the Chinese. On August 28 the Russians sent a note to all the powers in an attempt to alleviate their suspicions. The messages contended that St. Petersburg had "no designs of territorial acquisition in China," that its occupation of Manchuria was "for military purposes only," and that it intended eventually to remove its troops from the area.

It was obvious, however, that Russia would take an independent stand in the negotiations. Soon after the occupation of Peking the Russians declared that, since the Chinese court was no longer in Peking, there was no need to maintain troops or diplomatic representatives there and announced that they were withdrawing their forces and the Russian envoy to Tientsin. The other powers, fearing for the safety of all foreigners in Peking and suspecting

that St. Petersburg had made an arrangement with Li
Hung-chang in return for a free hand in Manchuria, refused
to support the Russian proposal. At the end of September
the Russian minister did leave Peking, but, because none of
the other diplomatic representatives followed his lead, he
returned on October 21.

The Russians were not the only source of discord in
allied capitals. A variety of issues, both petty and serious,
undermined any pretense of unity in the allied camp.
Virtually all the other powers resented the Germans because of their brutality and the somewhat overbearing
manner of Count von Waldersee, who behaved as if he had
supreme authority, though his authority over the other
commanders in Peking was more nominal than real. The
British had aroused suspicion for their activities in the
Yangtse Valley and were accused of shirking their share of
responsibility in the occupation of Peking. The Americans,
as always, tended to regard the machinations of the
European powers with a certain amount of disdain and
made it clear that they disapproved of the greedy behavior
of their erstwhile allies. In return, many of the Europeans
thought the United States flaunted its "special relationship" with China while at the same time sharing enthu-
siastically in the spoils of conquest.

As the time for negotiation approached, the allies
began to tire of the long and increasingly pointless occupation of north China. When they finally began to consider
the issues to be discussed, they could no longer avoid the
question of objectives. Despite the specific areas of disagreement among themselves—and there were many—the
allies found themselves in accord on a few basic issues in
the forthcoming negotiations: the Boxer leadership and
those government officials who had aided and abetted
their actions should be severely punished; the existing
treaty system between China and the powers, which had
been subject to criticism by various pressure groups in all
Western nations, should be revised; China should be compelled to pay the allies for the expenses they incurred during

the conflict and the ensuing occupation; China's military capacities should be reduced so that it would not be tempted to try again in the near future.

In November, in an effort to present a united front in the negotiations, the allies hammered out an eleven-point program. The major points included requirements that all Boxer elements and their supporters in the government be severely punished; a monument to the German envoy von Ketteler be erected in Peking; the legation quarter be secured against possible future attacks and protection for foreigners in China be improved; the importation of arms into China be limited for two years; the Taku forts be destroyed; and a modern foreign ministry be established to replace the existing Tsungli Yamen. Just before Christmas these items, plus an additional one—an apology to Japan for the murder of its diplomatic representative in Peking during the siege—were drawn up in a joint note and presented to the Chinese government. To save the face of the dynasty, the document was not presented in the form of a demand but was framed in such a way that the Chinese government would be able to carry out the various points on its own initiative.

The court in Sian submitted the program to the Grand Council for study. The council, under the direction of Jung Lu, who had been ordered to Sian from retirement at Li Hung-chang's insistence, recommended acceptance of most of the conditions. It appealed for leniency to all Manchu princes charged with complicity in the revolt (there were no legal grounds for the execution of high Manchu nobles) and for less severe limitations on the Chinese defense capacity. In particular, it asked permission to retain the forts at Taku on the grounds that they were vital to the defense of the capital. These suggestions were then transmitted to the Chinese negotiators for consideration.

The plenipotentiaries, however, were convinced that the allied program was not negotiable, and on December 27 they advised the court to accept the program in its entirety. The court capitulated and accepted the general

principles of the twelve-point program, directing the plenipotentiaries to attempt privately to soften the demands
along the lines suggested by the Grand Council. On January
10, 1901, the court formally agreed to sign the program,
and its signature was formally affixed to the document
six days later.

CHINESE RESPONSE TO THE PROGRAM

Well before the signing of the twelve-point program
the Chinese government had already begun to take actions
to meet the demands of the allies. In late September the
court had decreed on its own initiative that several high
officials—including Princes Tuan and Chuang, and Yü Hsien,
the governor of Shensi—be dismissed from office. Evidently
this was to be the extent of their punishment. To the
powers this gesture was totally inadequate. They insisted
that several high officials, including Prince Tuan and some
other militants, be executed, and they considered the
court's action to be a whitewash.

Throughout the autumn of 1900 the allies continued
to put pressure on the Chinese, declaring that they would
not agree to begin negotiations until proper punishments
had been meted out. Li Hung-chang added his own influence. He had been concerned about the predominance
of militants around the empress dowager in Sian, and it
was for this reason that he had recommended the return
of Jung Lu to the Grand Council. By the time Jung Lu had
arrived many of the militants had departed, and the Grand
Council was now dominated by moderates. Jung Lu immediately took charge and agreed to push for severe
punishments for those considered guilty by the allies.
Several of the more notorious antiforeign officials, including Yü Hsien, were to be banished for life. Others,
like Prince Tuan and other members of the high Manchu
nobility, were to be deprived of their rank and imprisoned.
Two of the leaders who had already taken their own lives—
Li Ping-heng and K'ang Yi—were to be dishonored post-

humously. The punishment of General Tung Fu-hsiang, however, was postponed. He was well liked in the area around Sian, and the court feared that riots might take place if he were dismissed from his military command.

The allies insisted, however, that the punishments proposed by the court were insufficient and demanded death sentences for those militants most reponsible for fomenting the crisis. There was some disagreement among the allies on how the sentences were to be carried out—the Germans, for instance, wanted the guilty parties turned over to the occupation authorities for punishment. Eventually the issue was left up to the Chinese government. When the court continued to temporize—Tz'u Hsi was obviously extremely reluctant to impose severe punishments on high Manchu officials—the allies finally agreed to compromise. Yü Hsien, perhaps the most hated of all by the foreigners, was beheaded. Prince Tuan was condemned to death, but on the agreement of the allies this sentence was commuted to banishment for life in far-off Sinkiang. Several others were allowed to commit suicide, and Tung Fu-hsiang was relieved of his command. By imperial decree, the reputations of those officials who had been executed for opposing the war were restored.

On other matters the court was somewhat more responsive to the demands of the allies. Provincial officials were informed by decree that they would be held personally responsible for the safety of all foreigners residing in the territory under their jurisdiction, while the Boxers and other similar secret organizations were declared illegal. All antiforeign activities were made punishable by death. Early in 1901 a new foreign ministry, called the *wai-wu-pu,* was established to replace the Tsungli Yamen. In a final gesture, the court accepted the allied demand for an indemnity of 450 million taels (about 67.5 million pounds or 190 million U.S. dollars). This figure had not been reached without disagreement among the allies. The United States had contended that the amount was too high and felt the figure should not exceed China's ability to pay. The other powers were more inclined toward severity, and eventually the United States withdrew its opposition. The court made a perfunctory attempt to reduce the figure to 400 million taels, but, when the allies appeared adamant, it accepted the original figure. The indemnity, to be paid off at four percent interest over thirty-one years, was divided into separate amounts for each power. Almost half of the total was comprised of claims by Germany and Russia. In 1908 the United States waived its claim on the understanding that the Chinese government would use the amount remaining for education.

The final protocol between China and the powers was initialed on September 7, 1901. By that time the fever of indignation in the West had passed, and China had already satisfied most of the demands in the final treaty. A formal apology was made to Germany and Japan for the assassination of their envoys, and a monument to the honor of von Ketteler was to be constructed in Peking at the expense of the Chinese government. Many of the Boxer leaders had been executed by the Chinese themselves, and the major court figures responsible for encouraging the uprising were either dead, in prison, or in exile. As a punishment to the scholar-gentry, many of whom had either supported the Boxers or stayed on the sidelines during the crisis, the civil service examinations, by which government officials had been recruited for over a thousand years, were suspended for five years in all cities where foreigners had been maltreated. China agreed to cease importing weapons for two years and to raze the forts at Taku. Finally, China consented to permit foreign powers to station guards within the legation quarter in Peking and ordered that all Chinese residents be evicted from the area.

THE TERRITORIAL ISSUE

Two questions, too complicated to be dealt with conclusively in the peace negotiations, still remained to be solved. One of the constant issues of Sino-foreign relations throughout the century had been trade. Many of the powers had hoped that the negotiations would result in treaty agreements for expanded trade between China and the outside world. The obstacle to fulfilling this hope was to be found less in China's position than among the allies themselves, for the latter continued to disagree over the issue. The British and Americans wanted to limit restrictions on open trading in China on the basis of the Open Door Notes of 1899. The Russians, in particular, wanted an economic monopoly in areas under their control. The issue was not resolved in 1900, nor would it be resolved in succeeding decades.

Unquestionably, the thorniest issue to emerge in the aftermath of the war was the territorial question. The Russian claims on Chinese territory became a *cause célèbre* that united most of the other powers in opposition. The first item to arise had been that of Russian claims on the land north of the Pei Ho at Tientsin "by right of conquest." The Russians successfully laid claim to a thousand acres along the north bank of the river across from the concessions area. The other powers soon followed suit. The British and French enlarged their existing concessions, and the Germans, the Japanese, and even the Austrians, Italians, and Belgians established their own. As usual, the American attitude was equivocal. The United States had possessed the right to a concession since 1861 but had not exercised this right. It now protested against the land grab of 1900 but would not formally abandon its own claim. Eventually the Americans arranged to have their own area combined with the British concession. What was less openly visible was less morally repugnant.

The seizure of concession land in Tientsin—more the result of follow-the-leader than of rational conviction—was hardly an effective way of coping with the broader threat of Russian expansion north of the Great Wall in Manchuria. Here there were serious grounds for anxiety. Rumors that a separate agreement existed between China and Russia circulated throughout the autumn of 1900, despite denials by both governments. Several powers energetically protested a separate peace arranged by any one of the allies, and the British invited Berlin to join in dissuading the Russians from unilateral action in China. For reasons of their own (one contemporary observer suggested that the kaiser was just playing a joke on the British), the Germans agreed to a joint four-point accord issued on October 16. The agreement declared that it was "a matter of joint and permanent international interest that the ports of China should remain free and open to trade and to every other legitimate form of economic activity for the nationals of all countries without distinction," an apparent reference to the growing Russian monopoly at Yingkow, in southern Manchuria. The two signatories agreed that they would not take advantage of Peking's present difficulties to seize additional territory in China and would exert joint efforts in "maintaining undiminished the territorial conditions of the Chinese empire." They pointedly invited other interested powers to maintain the conditions of the agreement.

The Anglo-German accord was in keeping with America's China policy as expressed in the Open Door Notes, and Washington replied that the agreement was consonant with its own policy in Asia. Several other powers—including France, Austria, Italy, and Japan—soon followed suit. The Russians, at whose territorial ambitions it was manifestly directed, responded coolly, stating that they had already indicated their compliance with the general spirit of the agreement.

The agreement had little effect on ensuing events. By early January word had leaked out of the Tseng-Alexeev Convention of the preceding November which suggested the extent of Russian demands. In that agreement Tseng had committed the Chinese government, without its knowledge, to allowing Russian construction of railroads in south Manchuria, dismantling Chinese military forts, and demobilizing all troops in the area. Yingkow and other strategic points were to be placed under Russian administration until the pacification of the area was completed.

The convention aroused an immediate storm of protest in China as well as abroad. Chinese officials were outraged that General Tseng had undertaken to sign an agreement so damaging in its implications for Chinese sovereignty in Manchuria. Among foreign powers, the Japanese were the most strongly hostile. They were not inclined to sit idly by while Russia consolidated its hold on all of Manchuria and north China.

While continuing to deny the existence of the agreement, the Russians attempted to obtain Chinese compliance by agreeing to minor modifications in the convention. The court was determined to resist but felt it was in a weak bargaining position without support from other powers. Formal negotiations between Russia and China began in early 1901. Yang Ju, minister at St. Petersburg, was designated as Chinese plenipotentiary (the Russsians considered him the most pliable choice), but he was directed to inform the court before consenting to any agreement.

In mid-January Finance Minister Witte presented Russian demands to Yang Ju. Considering the Russian proposals equivalent to the establishment of a protectorate in south Manchuria, Yang reported to the court his conviction that the Russians wanted virtually total power in Manchuria. He advised that negotiations be postponed to permit the Chinese government to solicit support from other powers. Li Hung-chang agreed, fearing that, if the Russian demands were accepted, the other foreign powers would themselves seize additional territory in self-defense. Li's maneuvers were only partly successful. The British (like the Germans, reluctant to antagonize St. Petersburg) and the Americans took little action, but Japan announced in a direct message to St. Petersburg that, if Russia claimed excessive concessions in Manchuria, other powers would have no alternative but to follow suit.

Under such pressure Witte reluctantly dropped his
demand that the Chinese government ratify the Tseng-
Alexeev Convention, and in February he presented a modi-
fied list of demands. Manchuria would be returned to
China, but Russia would obtain a monopoly of economic
rights in the area, as well as in Mongolia and Sinkiang.
Russia would have veto rights over the appointments of
Chinese commanders in the area and would be permitted
to construct a railway in the direction of Peking. If China
did not agree, Witte warned, the hard-liners in St. Petersburg
would demand the annexation of Manchuria.

For Li, of course, the only hope was to obtain support
from other interested nations. Britain joined Japan in its
concern and warned the Chinese government against consenting to any such agreement. Similar messages were sent
to the court by the viceroys in the center. But for Li the
problem was more complicated than his many advisers
realized. If China broke off negotiations now, the Russians
would simply remain in Manchuria, and the Chinese objective in the negotiations — Russia's agreement on a date
for departure — would not be realized.

It was clear to Li that only outside pressure could
persuade the Russians to leave without demanding extensive concessions in return. Li forcefully insisted to the
British and the Japanese that their protests should be
directed to St. Petersburg, not to Sian and Peking. For a
while he seemed to hesitate, and at one point appeared
ready to give in to St. Petersburg, but the court, itself
under pressure from lower officials and public opinion,
refused to accept the Russian demands and proposed re-
visions of its own. Yang Ju, caught in the middle and a
possible scapegoat in any eventuality, refused to resign if
the Russians did not agree to modify their demands.

When Witte agreed to drop references to Mongolia
and Sinkiang, Yang Ju and Li Hung-chang appeared satisfied, but the court still refused Russia's demands. This
refusal exasperated Li Hung-chang; he felt that the court

was overoptimistic about obtaining outside support. The Germans had already indicated that the Anglo-German agreement did not, in their interpretation, refer to Manchuria. Now, however, Chang Chih-tung had developed a backbone and contended that the loss of Manchuria would simply lead to the loss of the remaining eighteen provinces. To obtain support from the other powers, he suggested that the court open Manchuria to all nations, providing they aided China in resisting Russian demands. The court complied and then informed Yang Ju that he must make the final decision on whether or not to sign the accord.

Minister Yang Ju was now in an impossible position. Lacking real authority of his own, he would be blamed by patriots if he signed. If he refused, the Russian occupation of Manchuria would be on his shoulders. Li advised him to sign the agreement, but, aware of threats by the great powers to make demands of their own, Yang Ju refused to do so without express orders from the court.

By now the literate public in China was aroused. Telegrams poured in to the court calling for rejection of the accord. Abroad, Japan and Great Britain, aware of the gravity of the situation, offered their "full support" for the consequences if the Chinese refused to initial the agreement. The court—in an interesting argument from a government which supposedly did not make decisions in response to public opinion—announced that, since opinion at home and abroad was unanimously negative, it could not agree to Russian conditions. On March 23 it ordered Yang Ju not to sign the agreement and informed Russia through Li Hung-chang that no separate agreement could be reached prior to a collective agreement with all the allied powers.

At that point it was a war of nerves. China's belief that other nations would support its rejection of Russian demands seemed overly optimistic. Germany, the United States, and Great Britain were unlikely to act. France sympathized with the Russians. Japan was willing to run the risk of war to restrain Russian advances but could do little without support from other powers. Yet the bluff—if such it was—succeeded. Russia backed down and agreed to maintain the status quo without a separate agreement. No formal departure date for Russian troops had been set, but in April 1902 the Russians would agree to end their occupation of Manchuria.

On October 6, 1901, the court left Sian and returned to Peking, arriving in the capital on January 7, 1902. The city was just beginning to recover from the war. To force the removal of the allied occupation forces, the Chinese government had been compelled to accept humiliating conditions—punishment of its high officials, payment of reparations to the conquerors, destruction of its own defenses. Its armies had been ripped apart and bloodied, its citizens had been ravaged and despoiled. Unquestionably, the war was a costly one for China, in emotional as well as material terms.

Chinese responsibility for the conflict is not hard to demonstrate, but in the end the situation had developed into an allied slaughter. China was like an aging fighter who had challenged a younger, tougher foe. At the finish—with due respect to the foreigners still besieged in the legations—there was no contest, and the Chinese defeat reflected little credit on the allies. No accurate figures exist on the number of Chinese who died in the conflict, but their casualties were undoubtedly heavy. Not only regulars and Boxers, but innocent civilians were caught in the meat grinder of the allied advance to the capital. They died in countless ways—in allied bombardments, in direct combat, in massacres perpetrated by the soldiers of both sides. Some committed suicide. Prisoners were bayoneted by their captors, civilians were shot for sport, and Chinese laborers hired by the allies were shot simply for attempting to escape. For the modern observer, the disregard for human life, by both sides, was frightful.

At the time it was common in the West to cite the unspeakable atrocities committed by the Boxers, often with official support, against innocent missionaries in the provinces of China. That such evils did occur is undeniable. Yet the allied advance to Peking provided little in the way of contrast. In the end, neither side had much to be proud of. Indeed, in retrospect, the modern reader is justified in asking whether the Boxer Rebellion had any point at all.

Chapter Ten

The Legacy of
the Boxer Rebellion

To most contemporary observers in the West, the Boxer Rebellion was an irrational act—a primitive outburst by people who were ignorant of the destructive power of modern weapons and of the material and spiritual superiority of Western civilization over China's moribund culture. What else would explain the unshakable conviction of the court militants that China could go to war with all the advanced world powers at one time and emerge victorious? And how else could one understand the belief, held even by many educated Chinese, that the Boxer ritual had magical powers, or fathom the wild-eyed cruelty of those same Boxer hordes as they surged through the streets of Peking and other cities, searching out foreigners and their fellow travelers— the "second hairy ones"? Finally, what else would account for the contradictory policies of an aging sovereign who could send gifts of melons to the foreigners in the legation quarter while at the same moment expressing the wish "to sleep on their skins and eat their flesh"?

It is now clear that the truth was much more complex. The Boxer uprising was admittedly irrational and primitive. China had little hope of winning a struggle against the united efforts of all the great powers. Not only were its forces poorly armed and ill trained, but Chinese leaders were badly divided over the merits of the conflict and over the strategy of the dynasty itself. How could an ignorant mass of superstitious peasant youths rally the nation against the full power of Western imperialism?

Although contemporary observers were not entirely wrong in their assessment of the revolt, they had, nonetheless, missed the main point. In the broader perspective there was a method—often unconscious, to be sure—in the madness of this massive protest against the corrosive effects of the Western presence in China. To call this guiding principle nationalism would be to give it an intellectual quality which, for the most part, it did not possess. The resentment of the illiterate peasant against the Western missionary and of the village scholar against Western ideas and scientific innovations did not result from a clear consciousness of Chinese national identity. A true sense of nationalism implies an awareness of the world and the place of one's own homeland in it. In the nineteenth century most Chinese did not possess this vision of themselves and their role in the world of nations. Among the peasants, family loyalties and an emotional commitment to the village or the kin group took precedence over any sense of nationhood. Among the elite, a lingering view persisted of China as a culture rather than as a nation, and of China as the "Central Kingdom" in a Sinocentric universe. For many Chinese—and certainly for some of those who supported the Boxer uprising—the preservation of the cultural tradition was of equal, if not greater, importance than the survival of the Chinese nation itself. For the Manchu dynasty, nationalism as a phenomenon was suspect for the simple reason that the Manchus were a foreign ruling house, a people whose origins lay beyond the Great Wall.

As the end of the century approached, the aggressive behavior of the foreign imperialists had begun to make the

Chinese more conscious of themselves as a nation. But the process was not far advanced in 1900. The link between desperate peasants, naively claiming invulnerability to foreign bullets, and the militants at court anxious to evict troublesome foreigners from Chinese soil was very tenuous in that year of crisis. There was perhaps a primitive sense of throne and village fighting for a common destiny (certainly Tz'u Hsi herself viewed the conflict that way), but the Chinese people hardly saw themselves as involved in a deep-rooted, coherent struggle to preserve for China its rightful place in the world of nations. Looked at in this light, the Boxer Rebellion was not a clear expression of Chinese nationalism. For most Chinese that awareness was yet to come.

Nationalism, the most powerful primordial urge of our century, must be seen as a process, a dynamic social movement that begins with a small elite, often looking backward toward past glories rather than forward to a new vision of the future. Only gradually is such a movement transformed into a mature force involving the mass of the population. At the turn of the century Chinese nationalism was still an incoherent, almost formless phenomenon. It had roots in the reformist efforts of K'ang Yu-wei and his small coterie of followers; in the gut-deep hatred of the foreigner on the part of Li Ping-heng, Yü Hsien, and their countless unnamed counterparts throughout Chinese society; and even in the desperate, almost witless attempts of the court to turn peasant discontent into the spearhead of a vast social movement against Western imperialism in China. And its roots are found in the blind rage of the Boxer movement itself, which instinctively sought to solve the problems of the Chinese village by evicting unwanted foreign missionaries and their equally unwanted ideologies.

But the very diversity of the antiforeign movement was its weakness. The viceroys were as patriotic as the antiforeign militants, but they viewed the confrontation with the great powers as a grievous error which could lead to the fall of the dynasty, and they exerted their efforts to find a negotiated solution to the crisis. The reformists under K'ang Yu-wei were as concerned for the future of the nation as were the reactionaries at court, but they proposed radically different solutions to the crisis facing China. Thus no consensus existed as to how to deal with the Western challenge. Had Chinese society risen as one in a massive unified effort to evict the foreigner from Chinese soil, it is not impossible that, even without modern weapons, it could have been successful. But too many Chinese were convinced of the irrationality of violent resistance. Others believed that internal reform was the only effective way out of the national crisis.

In this perspective the Boxer Rebellion stands in Chinese history as a bridge between traditional antiforeignism and the emergence of modern nationalism, between a belief in the efficacy of Confucian solutions and a conviction that a new China must emerge. The Boxer Rebellion was the last stand of the old China, and it coincided with the birth of new forces which, in less than a generation, would begin the radical transformation of the age-old empire. In 1900 the traditionalist forces — the conservative court officials in Peking and the Confucian scholar-gentry in the countryside — were still dominant in China, and the Boxer Rebellion was their last desperate attempt to preserve the integrity of Chinese civilization without conceding the need for wholesale reforms in society. When they failed, the door was open for new men with new ideas to come to the fore.

Though the uprising failed, its effects on the future of China should not be underestimated. It undeniably exerted a tremendous catalytic force in spurring the evolution of nationalism in China. Although much of society stood aloof from direct participation in the uprising, the allied invasion and the foreign occupation of Peking, accompanied by the ignominious flight of the court to Sian, was a humiliating spectacle which could not easily be erased from the minds of millions of Chinese. The lesson to be learned was that the past policies of "muddling through" clearly would not work in the future.

The emotional consequences of the Boxer Rebellion were felt in many ways during the first decade of the new century. Russia's continued occupation of Manchuria, French expansion into Kwangsi and Yunnan, Western-controlled concession areas in the coastal cities, and the restrictive laws limiting Chinese immigration into the United States all inspired bitter resentment. This rising patriotic sentiment affected widely divergent sectors of Chinese society. New groups—students, merchants, government officials, soldiers—began to express patriotic attitudes and to demand that the dynasty do something to save China. Even the court showed a growing recognition that China had to modernize to survive. The blind traditionalism of the past was replaced by a cautious willingness to accept change, and in her declining years Tz'u Hsi put into effect many of the reforms originally suggested by K'ang Yu-wei during the abortive one hundred days in 1898.

This new mood was limited, however. Resistance to change was still deeply imbedded in Chinese society, and radicals frequently complained that appeals to their fellow countrymen went unheeded. The peasants, in particular, seemed to lapse back into quiescence. The writings of Chinese progressives during the early years of the new century were studded with frustrated references to the maddening indifference of the Chinese villager to the problems surrounding him in society. Nor was the dynasty's effort to revitalize China by piecemeal reforms a conspicuous success. Imperialism continued to nibble away at China's frontiers, particularly in the north, where the rivalry between Russia and Japan would intensify in the ensuing decades. Also, the court was unable to dampen the evangelical spirits of Western missionaries; the latter continued to arrive in large numbers as the new century began. The fact is, the Boxer Rebellion did not curb the voracious appetite of Western imperialism, which had increasingly powerful political and economic influence on China in succeeding decades.[1]

For the dynasty, the turn to virulent nationalism came too late, and, after Tz'u Hsi died in 1908 (her nephew, the still imprisoned Kuang Hsü, had died, significantly, the day before), the court seemed to lose its last breath of life. Its mainstays—Jung Lu, Li Hung-chang, Chang Chih-tung, Liu K'un-yi, and Tung Fu-hsiang—had all passed away, and nothing remained of the imperial government but an empty shell. In 1911 it was overthrown by revolutionaries under the leadership of Sun Yat-sen. Sun and his followers were strongly reform-minded, but they too failed to arrest the seeming decline of China, and thirty years later China was still struggling to restore control over its own destiny.

The decisive change occurred in 1949, when a new government came to power. This new government, like the Boxers, was fed by a deep, some would say irrational, hatred of the West and its legacy in China. Unlike the Boxers, however, if its emotional underpinnings were primitive, its understanding of the means to realize its goals was not. Under the charismatic leadership of Mao Tse-tung, it successfully drove all the imperialist wolves (Western and otherwise) from the gate and created a new measure of respect for China. It is no accident that the Chinese communists interpret the Boxer Rebellion as a positive force in the stirring of the Chinese masses against the ravages of foreign imperialism.[2] The rebellion, irrational and primitive in its impulses, was an integral stage in the emergence of nationalism in modern China. The movement had an elemental force that would be felt, not in mere days or months, but in years and generations.

The West understood little of the roots of the Boxer crisis and its potential meaning for the future of China. To the hardened imperialist, China was simply a source to exploit, a stamping ground for imperialist rivalry, incapable of handling its own affairs and therefore an inevitable victim of a universe designed on the principles of social Darwinism. Even those observers who had sympathy with the plight of China viewed it with an attitude of cultural condescension. An excerpt from an article by John Russell Coryell in *Harper's Weekly* is not atypical: "It has always seemed to me that the difficulty in understanding the Chinaman was chiefly the difficulty in obtaining a correct point of view. The mental processes of the average Chinese are those of a child. He is not taught to reason, and his education is a mere exercise in memory. He lacks background and perspective. If one would comprehend the attitude of the Chinese toward Western ideas, let him select the most ignorant person he can find and try to discuss a subtle ethical question with him. That question will be as comprehensible to him as an ordinary Western idea to the Chinaman."[3]

At best, China was seen as a laboratory for Westernization. In the memorable phrase of a now-forgotten American senator, the city of Shanghai was to be lifted up and ever up, until it reached the level of Kansas City. That the Chinese must go their own way, and that they must be allowed the breathing room to make their own choices, few could comprehend.

Of all the Western imperialist nations, the United States seemed the best prepared to understand the spirit of nascent nationalism and anti-imperialism which was beginning to animate the people of China. In 1900 most Americans still felt a healthy distrust of the grasping societies of the Old World and had an instinctive sympathy for China which survived even the widely publicized cruelties of the Boxer uprising. This attitude was clearly reflected in the policy of the McKinley administration, which, under the unruffled guidance of Secretary John Hay, was motivated by a sincere concern over the effects of the conflict on the territorial and administrative integrity of China. Throughout the crisis Washington attempted to take a conciliatory position which would permit the court in Peking to extricate itself from its position with a minimum of damage to its pride, and with its territory intact. While it is clear enough that the presidential campaign played a role in American policy, it is to the administration's credit that it resisted the temptation to use the emotional appeal of the besieged legations for political advantage.

Yet, although Washington exerted a major effort to preserve intact its independent policy toward China, the United States was inexorably drawn into the conflict by growing American interests in China. While many Americans were loath to admit it, the United States was becoming an increasingly active member of the Western imperialist club and was gradually coming to share its goals and its assumptions. Like their European counterparts, America's businessmen were in China to make money, and its missionaries to save souls. Expansionist forces throughout society were beginning to assert that the growing American stake in Asia demanded an active and expansionist foreign policy. They warned that hostile forces in Russia and Japan were waiting eagerly for an opportunity to absorb China into their own empires. Only the United States could save China from such a fate.

The contradiction between such attitudes and the tradition of nonentanglement in American foreign policy began to create a serious problem for the government in its effort to establish a coherent and independent policy toward China. In 1900 the expansionist forces were still relatively weak, and the McKinley administration was able to settle on an uneasy compromise. The United States joined the allied expeditionary force, but it reasserted its support for the preservation of the territorial and administrative integrity of the Chinese empire. China was to be punished for its actions, but not to the degree that it would irreparably harm its future prospects.

Yet the crisis had shown thoughtful Americans the questions to come. How would the United States balance its traditional concern for the rights of weak nations with its growing industrial and commercial interests throughout the world? At what point would America's sincere desire to promote the development of democratic institutions in Asia and its powerful moral urge to be a force for good in the world become an unwarranted interference in the internal affairs of other nations? At what point would American commercial and security interests begin to conflict with the legitimate aspirations of Asian nationalism? To what degree was it reasonable to expect other nations to follow the American model? These have not been easy questions to answer, and throughout the present century American foreign policy in Asia has vacillated sharply between indifference and involvement. Since World War II, of course, a spirit of interventionism has predominated, driven by the dual forces of economic need and moral concern. The culmination came in Vietnam, when the imperatives of our own apparent foreign-policy requirements blinded us to the realities of a small Asian nation motivated by forces which we did not understand. In the aftermath of our smarting defeat in Saigon in 1975, we are now searching uneasily for a middle ground, for a foreign policy which can reflect our own legitimate national interests without unnecessarily infringing on the rights of others.

Across the distance of time, then, a kinship exists between ourselves and the generation that watched the events of the Boxer Rebellion unfold, a common need to understand the aspirations of our neighbors across the sea. Today, as then, we are pulled by contradictory impulses, and the road to a solution is murky and pitted with obstacles. Today, as then, China's hostility to the West runs deep, and mutual suspicion and misunderstanding mark the relationship. In 1900 our predecessors were optimistic for a "Western solution" in China. Today we are sadder, but perhaps wiser, and are more willing to tolerate a solution acceptable to the Chinese people themselves. For that, if for that alone, we may feel that we have taken a step forward in unraveling the tangled relations between China and the West.

Notes

CHAPTER ONE
WORLDS IN COLLISION

1. The best all-around treatment of China's traditional role in Asia is the collection of essays entitled *The Chinese World Order* (Cambridge: Harvard University Press, 1968), edited by John K. Fairbank. For an interesting discussion of traditional foreign policy from a Chinese point of view, see Kuo-chi Lee, *Chang Chih-tung ti Wai-chiao cheng-ts'e* [Chang Chih-tung's Foreign Policy] (Taipei: Academia Sinica, 1970), pp. 127-37.
2. This letter is quoted in Ssu-yu Teng and John K. Fairbank, *China's Response to the West* (New York: Atheneum, 1963), pp. 24-28.
3. The British attitude toward the missionary effort is competently explored in Edmund S. Wehrle's *Britain, China, and the Anti-missionary Riots, 1891-1900* (Minneapolis: University of Minnesota Press, 1966).

CHAPTER TWO
THE CLIMAX OF IMPERIALISM IN CHINA

1. *Harper's Weekly* (September 22, 1900), p. 885.
2. Andrew Malozemoff, *Russian Far Eastern Policy, 1881-1904* (Berkeley: University of California Press, 1958), p. 122.

CHAPTER THREE
THE RISE OF THE BOXERS

1. Quoted in Tai Hsüan-chih, *I Ho T'uan Yen-chiu* [A Study of the Boxers] (Taipei: Commercial Press, 1963), p. 57.
2. George N. Steiger, *China and the Occident* (New Haven: Yale University Press, 1927).
3. A good discussion of this issue is Jerome Ch'en's "The Origin of the Boxers," Jerome Ch'en and Nicholas Tarling, eds., *Social History of China and Southeast Asia* (Cambridge: Cambridge University Press, 1970), pp. 57-84.
4. *Foreign Relations of the United States (1900)* (Washington: Government Printing Office, 1902), p. 84.

CHAPTER FOUR
THE CRISIS ESCALATES

1. Paul H. Clements, *The Boxer Rebellion: A Political and Diplomatic Review* (New York: Columbia Press, 1915), pp. 105-6.
2. Hosea Ballou Morse, *The International Relations of the Chinese Empire* (London: Longman's Green, 1910-18), vol. 3, p. 186.
3. The French attitude is clearly expressed in French foreign affairs documents held at the Quai d'Orsay in Paris.
4. The diverse personalities of the diplomatic figures in Peking are described in several accounts and memoirs of the period. Some of the more prominent are B. L. Putnam Weale (pseudonym of Bertram Simpson), *Indiscreet Letters from Peking* (New York: Dodd, Mead, 1922); Mary Hooker (pseudonym of Polly Condit Smith), *Behind the Scenes in Peking* (London: J. P. Murray, 1910); and Lancelot Giles, *The Siege of the Peking Legations: A Diary* (Nedlands: Western Australia Press, 1970). A more recent account which gives vivid portrayals of the *dramatis personae* is Richard O'Connor's *The Spirit Soldiers: A Historical Narrative of the Boxer Rebellion* (New York: G. P. Putnam's Sons, 1973).
5. *Foreign Relations of the United States (1900)*, p. 143.
6. The best English-language source for information on the situation at court is Chester Tan's *The Boxer Catastrophe* (New York: Columbia University Press, 1955). Another source, which should be used with care, is Ching-shan's *The Diary of His Excellency Ching-shan* (Leiden: E. J. Brill, 1924), J. J. L. Duyvendak trans.; many scholars question the veracity of the latter account which some allege is composed of selections from diaries of other court personages and—in some cases—of complete fabrications. I have turned to the *Diary* for background purposes only. For a discussion, see *the Boxer Uprising*, Appendix A, pp. 272–84.

7. Cited in George Lynch, *The War of the Civilizations, Being the Record of a "Foreign Devil's" Experiences with the Allies in China* (New York: Longman's Green, 1901), p. 122. This is an extraordinarily good source for the allied intervention in north China.
8. O'Connor, p. 95.
9. Lynch, pp. 124-25.

CHAPTER FIVE
THE INTERNATIONAL DETACHMENTS

1. The standard account of the modernization of the Chinese army at the turn of the century is Ralph Powell's *The Rise of Chinese Military Power, 1895-1912* (Port Washington, N.Y.: Kenniket Press, 1955). Another useful source is Henry Purcell's *The Boxer Uprising: A Background Study* (London: Cambridge University Press, 1963).
2. A detailed discussion of their attitudes can be found in Tai Hsüan-chih, especially pages 115-31. For Chang Chih-tung's views and behavior, see Lee Kuo-chi, *Chang Chih-tung*, Chapter 3.
3. Lee Kuo-chi, p. 142.
4. The most detailed accounts of the Seymour expedition are given in H. C. Thomson, *China and the Powers: A Narrative of the Outbreak of 1900* (New York: Longman's Green, 1902); Henry Savage-Landor, *China and the Allies* (London: Heinemann, 1901); and Arthur Smith, *China in Convulsion* (New York, 1901).
5. Tan, p. 72.
6. A translation of the text is in Ching-shan, pp. 75-76.
7. The earlier decision had been made in 1860, during the allied invasion of north China.
8. *Leslie's Weekly* (August 11, 1900), p. 107.
9. Cited in Morse, vol. 3, p. 227.

CHAPTER SIX
THE SIEGE OF PEKING

1. Giles, p. 115.
2. Ching-shan, p. 44.
3. B. L. Putnam Weale, p. 110; cited in O'Connor, pp. 162-63.
4. There is much controversy about this alleged decree, said to have been issued on June 24. It is mentioned in Ching-shan, p. 50. Some students of the period, however, are skeptical about the existence of the decree.
5. Sources on her life include Princess Der Ling, *Old Buddha* (New York: Dodd, Mead, 1928), and Harry Hussey, *Venerable Ancestor:*

The Life and Times of Tz'u Hsi (1835-1908) Empress of China (New York: Doubleday, 1949).

CHAPTER SEVEN
THE BATTLE OF TIENTSIN

1. Hoover's memoirs are an interesting source for the siege at Tientsin. Herbert Hoover, *Memoires* (New York: MacMillan, 1951).
2. Lynch, pp. 19-20.
3. An interesting account of the battle of Tientsin is Richard Weinert's "The Battle of Tientsin," in *American History Illustrated* (November 1966).
4. Leland Smith, a photographer attached to the unit, visited the area shortly after the battle and, according to his recollection seventy years later, "the whole area where the regiment was placed was under direct view of the Chinese on the Wall just across the river." Smith said he "was astonished that anyone got out." Leland Smith papers, Signal Corps Collection, *Spanish-American War Survey*, Archives, Military History Research Center (MHRC).
5. For an account of the post-battle looting, see Savage-Landor, vol. 1, pp. 199, 201.

CHAPTER EIGHT
THE ADVANCE TO PEKING

1. *Foreign Relations of the United States (1900)*, p. 260.
2. *Ibid.*, p. 294.
3. Paul Cambon to Paris (12 July 1900), in *Politique Etrangère (Chine): Relations avec les Puissances*, NS 100 (7-14 July 1900), p. 157.
4. Besides Thomson, Lynch, and Savage-Landor, other accounts of the advance to Peking are Weinert's "The Capture of Peking," in *American History Illustrated* (January 1968); Frederick Brown, *From Tientsin to Peking with the Allied Forces* (New York: Arno Press, 1970); and A. S. Daggett, *America in the China Relief Expedition* (Kansas City: Hudson-Kimberly, 1903).
5. According to one survivor of the war, Chaffee was a strong advocate of an early advance, announcing to his fellow commanders, "I am going to Peking and you can come along if you want." Leland Smith papers, Archives, MHRC.
6. For a recent account of the battle by a participant, see the recollections in David Burr Hight papers, *Spanish-American War Survey*, Archives, MHRC. According to Hight, General Gaselee had originally estimated that the allies would require two days to take Yangts'un. Chaffee had retorted, "Put the Americans in the

front lines and we'll take it in two hours." The objective was achieved in an hour and a half. Hight's papers are also a good source for comments on the weather conditions on the march.
7. Lynch, p. 246. By all accounts the Russian soldiers were most guilty of atrocities on the march. As one American participant commented, "These Russians are sure the scum." Leland Smith papers, Archives, MHRC.
8. Giles, p. 178.

CHAPTER NINE
THE AFTERMATH

1. The most detailed account in English on the post-war negotiations is Tan, *The Boxer Catastrophe*. For a Chinese account, see Tai Hsüan-chih, *I Ho Tu'an Yen-chiu*, Chapter VIII.
2. When von Waldersee attempted to assert his command over all allied troops in the capital area, General Chaffee responded heatedly, "I am commander of the American troops and will give all orders necessary to my own men." Leland Smith papers, Archives, MHRC.

CHAPTER TEN
THE LEGACY OF THE BOXER REBELLION

1. It is only fair to point out that many recent students contend that the dynasty's foreign policy became somewhat more effective after 1900. For example, see John Schrecker, *Imperialism and Chinese Nationalism: Germany in Shantung* (Cambridge: Harvard University Press, 1971).
2. For a discussion, see James P. Harrison, *The Communists and Chinese Peasant Rebellions: A Study in the Rewriting of Chinese History* (New York: Atheneum, 1969).
3. *Harper's Weekly* (September 29, 1900), p. 920.

Selected Bibliography

DOCUMENTARY SOURCES

Foreign Relations of the United States. Washington: Government Printing Office, 1900-1901.

Etat Numerique des Fonds de la Correspondance Politique et Commerciale, 1897-1918, Dossiers Générales, August 1898-October 1900. Ministère des Affaires Etrangères, Politique Etrangère (Chine) Relations avec les Puissances, July 1899-December, 1900 (NS 96-NS 113). *Spanish-American War Survey*, Archives, Military History Research Center (MHRC).

BOOKS AND ARTICLES

———. *I Ho T'uan* [The Boxers] . 3 vols. Shanghai, 1961.

Bland, J. O. P., and Backhouse, E. *China under the Empress Dowager, Being the History of the Life and Times of Tzu Hsi.* London: Heinemann, 1911.

Brown, Frederick. *From Tientsin to Peking with the Allied Forces.* New York: Arno Press and the New York Times, 1970.

Butler, Smedley. *Old Gimlet Eye.* New York: Farrar & Rinehart, 1933.

Ch'en Jerome, *Yüan Shih-k'ai.* Palo Alto: Stanford University Press, 1972.

———. "The Origin of the Boxers." In *Social History of China and Southeast Asia,* edited by Jerome Ch'en and Nicholas Tarling. London: Cambridge University Press, 1970.

Ching-shan. *The Diary of His Excellency Ching-shan, Being A Chinese Account of the Boxer Troubles.* Translated by J. J. L. Duyvendak. E. J. Brill, 1924.

Clymer, Kenton J. *John Hay: The Gentleman as Diplomat.* Ann Arbor: University of Michigan Press, 1975.

Daggett, A. S. *America in the China Relief Expedition.* Kansas City: Hudson-Kimberly, 1903.

Dennett, Tyler. *John Hay: From Poetry to Politics.* Port Washington, N.Y.: Kenniket Press, 1963.

Der Ling, Princess. *Old Buddha.* New York: Dodd, Mead, 1928.

Des Forges, Roger. *Hsi Liang and the Chinese National Revolution.* New Haven: Yale University Press, 1973.

Fairbank, John K. *The Chinese World Order.* Cambridge: Harvard University Press, 1968.

Giles, Lancelot. *The Siege of the Peking Legations: A Diary.* Edited and with an introduction by L. R. Marchant. Nedlands: Western Australia Press, 1970.

Harrison, James P. *The Communists and Chinese Peasant Rebellions: A Study in the Rewriting of Chinese History.* New York: Atheneum, 1969.

Hummell, Arthur. *Eminent Chinese of the Ch'ing Period.* Washington: Government Printing Office, 1943.

Hussey, Harry. *Venerable Ancestor: The Life and Times of Tz'u Hsi (1835-1908) Empress of China.* New York: Doubleday, 1949.

Iriye, Akira, *Across the Pacific.* New York: Harcourt, Brace & World, 1967.

Lee, Kuo-chi. *Chang Chih-tung ti wai-chiao cheng-ts'e* [Chang Chih-tung's Foreign Policy] Taipei: Academia Sinica, 1970.

Lensen, George Alexander. *The Russo-Chinese War.* Tallahassee: Diplomatic Press, 1967.

Lynch, George. *The War of the Civilizations, Being the Record of a "Foreign Devil's" Experiences with the Allies in China.* New York: Longman's Green, 1901.

Malozemoff, Andrew. *Russian Far Eastern Policy, 1881-1904.* Berkeley: University of California Press, 1958.

May, Ernest R., and Thomson, James C., Jr. *American-East Asian Relations: A Survey.* Cambridge: Harvard University Press, 1972.

McClellan, Robert. *The Heathen Chinee: A Study of American Attitudes toward China, 1890-1905.* Columbus: Ohio State University, 1971.

Morse, Hosea Ballou. *The International Relations of the Chinese Empire.* 3 vols. London: Longman's Green, 1910-18.

O'Connor, Richard. *The Spirit Soldiers: A Historical Narrative of the Boxer Rebellion.* New York: G. P. Putnam's Sons, 1973.

Pelcovits, Nathan. *Old China Hands and the Foreign Office.* New York: King's Crown Press, 1948.

Powell, Ralph. *The Rise of Chinese Military Power, 1895-1912.* Port Washington, N.Y.: Kenniket Press, 1955.

Purcell, Henry. *The Boxer Uprising: A Background Study.* London: Cambridge University Press, 1963.

Savage-Landor, Henry. *China and the Allies.* London: Heinemann, 1901.

Schrecker, John. *Imperialism and Chinese Nationalism: Germany in Shantung.* Cambridge: Harvard University Press, 1971.

Smith, Arthur. *China in Convulsion.* New York: F. H. Revell, 1901.

Spence, Jonathan. *To Change China: Western Advisers in China, 1620-1960.* Boston: Little, Brown, 1969.

Tai, Hsüan-chih. *I Ho T'uan Yen-chiu* [A Study of the Boxers]. Taipei: Commercial Press, 1963.

Tan, Chester. *The Boxer Catastrophe.* New York: Columbia University Press, 1955.

Thomson, H. C. *China and the Powers: A Narrative of the Outbreak of 1900.* New York: Longman's Green, 1902.

Wehrle, Edmund S. *Britain, China, and the Anti-missionary Riots, 1891-1900.* Minneapolis: University of Minnesota Press, 1966.

Weinert, Richard. "The Battle of Tientsin." In *American History Illustrated.* (November 1966), pp. 8-13, 52-55.

———. "The Capture of Peking." In *American History Illustrated* (January 1968), pp. 22-28.

Wilson, James Harrison. *Under the Old Flag.* New York: Appleton, 1912.

Wu Yung. *The Flight of an Empress.* New Haven: Yale University Press, 1936.

Varg, Paul. *The Making of a Myth: the U.S. and China, 1897-1912.* East Lansing: Michigan State University Press, 1968.

Young, Marilyn Blatt. *The Rhetoric of Empire: American China Policy, 1895-1901.* Cambridge: Harvard University Press, 1968.

Index

223

Since 1967 William J. Duiker has been an associate professor of history and director of International Program Development for the College of Liberal Arts at The Pennsylvania State University. He is currently Chairman of the Vietnam Studies Group of the Association for Asian Studies. He is also a member of Phi Alpha Theta Honor Society in History. His previous books include: *The Rise of Nationalism in Vietnam, 1900–1941,* and *Ts'ai Yuan-p'ei: Educator of Modern China.*